The Last Word

What Revelation Says about Today's Troubled Times

Stan Key

Stan Key

Rev. 12:11

Warner Press

Warner Press Inc.
Anderson, Indiana 46012

Published by Warner Press Inc.
Warner Press and the "WP" logo are trademarks of Warner Press Inc.

Warner Press Inc.
PO Box 2499
Anderson, IN 46018-2499
800-741-7721
www.warnerpress.org

ISBN: 978-1-59317-795-9

Printed in the United States of America.

TABLE OF CONTENTS

Introduction

Ever since I was a child, I've loved books with pictures. There is just something about pages and pages of text that intimidates me. But with pictures, the story comes alive. If you like picture books, then I have one for you: the New Testament book of Revelation! I don't mean you will find actual sketches or paintings in it, but you will find lots of word-pictures. When you read this book, all sorts of fascinating images come to life. In fact, to read this book properly, you'll need a sanctified imagination! Consider some of the word-pictures encountered in Revelation:

- Dragons, beasts, and ten-headed monsters
- Angel armies
- Four horsemen bringing death and destruction
- Plagues of global dimensions
- Two cities: Jerusalem, holy and eternal, and Babylon, wicked and doomed
- A wedding of cosmic proportions
- Mortal combat between a Dragon and a Lamb

Revelation introduces us to a world "in which children are instinctively at home and in which adults, by becoming as little children, recapture an elemental involvement in the basic conflicts and struggles that permeate moral existence."[1] Revelation is like no other book in the Bible. Little wonder that many Christians have avoided its unfamiliar terrain.

The great theme of the book of Revelation is the triumph of the Lamb. In cosmic conflict with the Dragon, the Lamb has wounds. In fact, it has been slain, but by a miracle of God, the Lamb has been brought back to life and is now standing in the center of God's throne in heaven! In company with Almighty God and the Holy Spirit, all creation bows in worship before him.

---

1 Eugene H. Peterson, *Reversed Thunder: The Revelation of John & the Praying Imagination* (San Francisco: HarperCollins, 1991), x.

"Worthy is the Lamb who was slain, to receive power and wealth and wisdom and might and honor and glory and blessing!" (Rev 5:12)

A good storyteller is not supposed to reveal the conclusion of the story until the last chapter, but the author of Revelation simply can't keep it a secret: *the Lamb wins!* In fact, he tells us in the very first chapter that the outcome of this conflict was determined before the foundation of the world.

Revelation not only describes cosmic characters in heaven but also introduces us to earthly ones, most notably two women: a great *Prostitute* who symbolizes Babylon, the city of man (she worships wealth, power, and sensual pleasures), and a pure *Virgin*, who represents the church (she is being prepared for her wedding day when she will marry the Lamb). The book of Revelation confronts us with the sobering reality that every human being belongs to one of these women, either the Prostitute or the Virgin. Because these women represent two cities, Babylon and Jerusalem, the book causes you and me to ask a life-defining question: with which city does my citizenship lie?

Finding the Right Approach

To fully appreciate the book of Revelation, we need to recognize its literary form. From about 200 BC to AD 100, a new genre of Jewish writing appeared called "apocalyptic literature" (from the Greek term *apokalupsis*, meaning "unveiling" or "revealing"). These writings sought to inspire hope for God's people in the midst of great adversity. This literature used dramatic symbolism and prophetic visions and tended to highlight certain distinctive themes:

1. We live in the midst of a cosmic conflict between good and evil.
2. Understanding God's plan for the future enables us to survive the tribulations we face today.
3. Though it may not appear from outward circumstances to be the case, God is in control of human history.

The biblical books of Revelation and Daniel clearly belong to this type of literature. However, Revelation, being a distinctively Christian book, goes beyond the Jewish apocalyptic genre in several important ways, making it unique:

1. The writer of Revelation calls his book a prophecy (see 1:3; 22:7, 10, 18, 19).
2. The writers of Jewish apocalyptic books nearly always used fanciful pseudonyms, but the book of Revelation identifies its author as a historical person: John (see 1:4, 9; 22:8).
3. Jewish apocalyptic literature was generally pessimistic about the present age, but Revelation maintains a balanced realism of hope for God's people in the midst of current trials (see John 16:33).
4. Most apocalyptic literature focused solely on the future, but the book of Revelation has a strong moral message for today (a call to repentance and faithfulness).
5. The apostle John, the one traditionally identified as the author of Revelation, left a body of other writings (three pastoral letters and a Gospel) that give us a more complete understanding of his message; other apocalyptic writers did not.

Over the centuries, Bible students have taken four basic interpretive approaches to the book of Revelation.

The *contemporary-historical approach* assumes that John is writing about events occurring in the first century. Thus, the Beast is typically seen as a specific Roman emperor; the Great Prostitute as Rome, etc. This approach assumes that most of the book's prophecies would have been fulfilled within the lifetime of the author. The primary problem with this view is that the overwhelming victory portrayed in the latter chapters of Revelation did not occur during the lifetime of John or his contemporaries—in fact, it still has not occurred.

The *historicist approach* holds that Revelation is a prediction of events from the writer's day to our own—and beyond. The reader of Revelation, therefore, examines the book looking for parallels in the centuries of church history (the Reformation, the French Revolution, the reestablishment of the nation of Israel, etc.). The weakness of this approach is seen in the fact that few interpreters can agree on which historical event is foreshadowed by each symbol in the book of Revelation.

The *futurist approach* is currently the most popular understanding of Revelation, serving as the basis for many widely known books and commentaries and the Left Behind novel series. The basic idea is that everything after Revelation 4:1 points to events still in the future. According to this view, most of the book was written to help Christians of the future prepare for the return of Christ. This method of interpretation often assumes that the seven churches mentioned in chapters 2–3 represent seven successive stages of church history leading up to the supposed Rapture of the church seen to occur in 4:1. The weakness of this view is that it means the book of Revelation would have had little significance for the readers who received it in the first century. Furthermore, there is almost no textual reason to see the seven churches as typifying seven successive ages of history.

The *idealist approach* claims that the book does not refer to any specific historical events or time periods at all. Rather, it is a book of spiritual symbolism, a kind of theological poem that expresses the ageless conflict between the Kingdom of Light and the Kingdom of Darkness. The weakness of this approach is that parts of Revelation seem to have a clear historical reference (see 1:9; 2:1–3:22; 17:9).

Though mysteries certainly remain about how Revelation should be best interpreted, there is little indication that John intended his book to be used as a kind of crystal ball or Ouija board to help the curious predict future events. Transforming the book into charts and timelines that map out a chronology of future world events may reveal the creative genius of the interpreter, but such an approach seems to miss the point of John's original purpose in writing. After examining the various interpretive approaches, Robert H. Mounce sums up the matter by saying, "It is readily apparent that each approach has some important contribution to a full understanding of Revelation and that no single approach is sufficient in itself."[2]

John wrote as a pastor, not as a Christian futurist. He wrote to help believers in the churches of Asia survive and thrive as they lived in the evil empire of first-century Rome. His words often have an obvious future reference and certainly reassured those first-century Christians of the final victory of the Lamb of God. But his pastoral counsel has application for all believers everywhere and at all times—whether they live under Nero, Attila the Hun, Adolf Hitler, Idi Amin, or anyone else. Simply put, the book of Revelation is not a codebook to decipher the future but an invitation to trust in the Lamb.

Why Study Revelation?

For many years I avoided the book of Revelation. For me, it felt like a closed book, impossible to understand. I was dismayed by how I saw others handle it and concluded that I should just steer clear of this enigmatic book. Later in life, however, I began to think differently. I began to warm to this wonderful book and see truths that ministered deeply to my troubled soul. I even preached an 18-sermon series to the congregation I pastored. Let me explain why.

The book of Revelation is an *understandable* word. Don't believe the hucksters who say that Revelation is written in obscure code language so that only people with special training or some mystical gift of discernment can decipher it. When it was read aloud to worshipers in the seven churches of the first century, they apparently understood its meaning. We can too. Therefore, "Do not seal up the words of the prophecy of this book, for the time is near" (22:10).

The book of Revelation is a *pastoral* word. Note that the whole book is addressed to the seven churches in the province of Asia (1:4). In all

---

2 Robert H. Mounce, *The Book of Revelation: The New International Commentary of the New Testament, Revised* (Grand Rapids: Eerdmans, 1997), 43.

probability, John was their pastor or bishop or, at the very least, one of a team of persons providing oversight and pastoral care. So when John writes of a beast, angelic trumpets, and worldwide plagues, he is not writing as a speculative theologian. He is writing as a shepherd concerned for his sheep! The book was written to encourage Christians living under the oppression of Rome, and it must be interpreted in that light. We might call the book of Revelation a *Survivor's Guide to Life in Babylon*. It describes how to live victoriously in a world of temptation, persecution, false doctrine, apostasy, demonic influences, and constant pressure to conform to the secular culture by saying, "Caesar is lord."

Revelation is also a *blessed* word. John enumerates a sevenfold benediction for believers, especially for those who read it and do what it says:

1. "Blessed is the one who reads aloud the words of this prophecy, and blessed are those who hear, and who keep what is written in it…" (1:3).

2. "Blessed are the dead who die in the Lord from now on…that they may rest from their labors, for their deeds follow them!" (14:13).

3. "Blessed is the one who stays awake, keeping his garments on, that he may not go about naked and be seen exposed!" (16:15).

4. "Blessed are those who are invited to the marriage supper of the Lamb…" (19:9).

5. "Blessed and holy is the one who shares in the first resurrection! Over such the second death has no power, but they will be priests of God and of Christ, and they will reign with him for a thousand years" (20:6).

6. "Blessed is the one who keeps the words of the prophecy of this book" (22:7).

7. "Blessed are those who wash their robes, so that they may have the right to the tree of life and that they may enter the city by the gates" (22:14).

Perhaps we should admit to an ulterior motive in studying this book: we want to share in the blessing!

The book of Revelation is a *final* word. Last words are important, and with this book, God's revelation to humanity is complete. Christian scripture ends here. When Pastor John put down his quill after writing "Amen" at the end of chapter 22, God had finished speaking. Though he was still active in the world, he had said everything he intended to say. Nothing needed to be added. Nothing needed to be taken away. There will be no further revelation from God until the heavens open, a white horse appears, and one named "The Word of God" (19:13) comes to judge the nations. Because it is final, anyone who adds to or takes from this word is cursed (see 22:18–19).

> *What more can he say, than to you he has said,*
> *To you who for refuge to Jesus have fled?*[3]

We should realize, however, that for John the "word" (Gk. *logos*) is not simply a spoken sound or a written document. In its ultimate expression, God's final Word is Jesus Christ (see John 1:1, 14). This helps us to understand why John refers to his book as "the revelation of Jesus Christ" (1:1). This final book of the New Testament is not just a revelation *from* Jesus Christ. It is a revelation *of* Jesus Christ. The preposition is important. The book is not only mediated *by* (*from*) Jesus, it is an unveiling *of* Christ himself in all of his glory and power. The purpose of God's final Word is not just that we know about the future, but that we know the Lord of the future!

> He who testifies to these things says, "Surely I am coming soon." Amen. (Rev 22:20)

---

3 "How Firm a Foundation," from *A Section of Hymns,* by John Rippon (1787), attributed variously to John Keene, Kirkham, or John Keith.

The word *amen* comes from a Hebrew term meaning "firm, dependable, trustworthy, certain, and true." Anyone who says "amen" to a prayer or doxology shows agreement with what has been said and affirms it as the hearer's own. "So be it...May it be true..." Thus, it is fitting that the last word of the book of Revelation is an invitation for all of us to affirm our personal faith in the Lamb for all that he is, all that he has done, and all that he will yet accomplish in the future: "The grace of the Lord Jesus be with all. Amen" (22:21).

Revelation Outline

1. Introduction (1:1–20)
2. Letters to the seven churches (2:1–3:22)
3. Heavenly vision of the Lamb (4:1–5:14)
4. The seven seals (6:1–7:17)
5. The seven trumpets (8:1–11:19)
6. War between good and evil (12:1–14:20)
7. The seven last plagues (15:1–16:21)
8. The fall of Babylon (17:1–19:21)
9. The millennial reign and final judgment (20:1–15)
10. A new heaven, new earth, and new Jerusalem (21:1–22:5)
11. Epilogue (22:6–21)

How to Study Revelation

This book is the revelation *of* Jesus Christ written by a pastor to suffering Christians living in an evil empire about "things that must soon take place" (1:1). As you study each passage, ask yourself,

- How does this passage reveal Jesus Christ?
- How does this passage give me strength and comfort when I confront evil today?
- How does this passage give me hope for tomorrow?

1.

The One Who Holds the Keys

(Rev 1:1-20)

The 2006 movie *Night at the Museum*[4] takes place in the Museum of Natural History in New York City, where something strange is going on. At night, when the museum is closed, all the wax figures and stuffed animals come to life. This poses a real challenge for the night watchman, whose job is to keep order during the night. In one scene, a little monkey and the night watchman are fighting over the watchman's keys. They both understand one thing very clearly: whoever has the keys controls the museum. The one who holds the keys wins!

We might say the book of Revelation is based on the same understanding. Surveying the entire sweep of human history, John tells us who is holding the keys—the keys to death and Hades, as well as the keys to eternity! The one who holds the keys controls everything: what happened in John's time, what is happening in our own time, and what will happen in the future. But who is the one who holds the keys?

The Greek word *apocalypsis*, which our Bible translates as *revelation,* means an "unveiling" or "uncovering," making something known that was not known before. What John is uncovering in this wonderful book is not just the end of the world, but Jesus himself. To understand this book correctly, it is indispensable that we understand that John's primary purpose in writing is to reveal Jesus Christ, the one who holds the keys!

Read the prologue of the book of Revelation (see 1:1–3), and you will find that the origin and nature of the book is all told in the prepositions. This revelation or "unveiling" is *from* God, mediated *through* an angel,

---

4 Robert Ben Garant and Thomas Lennon, "Night at the Museum" (2006), directed by Shawn Levy.

given *to* John (who is to share it with the churches—and with us), and it is *of* Jesus. This book is not just about future events. Preeminently, it is an "unveiling" of Jesus, his identity and work (past, present, and future). The prologue also promises a blessing to the one who *reads* this book aloud, to the one who *hears* what is read, and to the one who *does* what it tells us to do.

We may wonder why God's angel declares, "The time is near" (v 3), a statement echoed by Christ himself at the end of the book when he says, "I am coming soon" (22:7, 12, 20). These statements were made about nineteen hundred years ago! In what sense is the glorious victory of Jesus Christ and the coming Kingdom "near"? In what sense is Jesus' return "soon"? You can be sure that we who read the book of Revelation today are not the first to wonder *when* the end will come. Even in the New Testament era, Jesus' followers frequently asked this important question (see Mark 13:4; Acts 1:6–7; 1 Thess 5:1–11; 2 Pet 3:8–10).

Christ's coming changed the way God's people think about the End. During Christ's earthly ministry, time was normally conceived as having two stages:

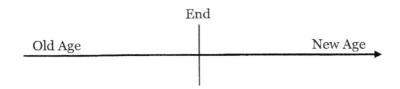

But Jesus' teaching changed this perspective so that his followers now understand that time looks like this:

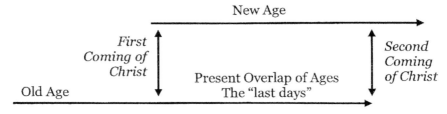

Christians now live in an era "in between." We are called to live victoriously in the interval between the old age and the age to come (the two comings of Christ), between the promise of God and the fulfillment of that promise, between the "already" and the "not yet." Living in the land of "in between" is not easy. It wasn't easy for the Christians in the first century, and it isn't easy for us today. Some have likened this time to the months between D-Day and the Battle of Berlin in World War II. The Allied invasion at Normandy meant that the fall of the Third Reich was "already" a reality, but its consummation was "not yet." Though the outcome was certain, the time "in between" was filled with drama and danger.

In verses 4–8, John sends pastoral greetings to seven churches in what is now Turkey. Because John is a pastor writing to his flock, it is legitimate to see the entire book of Revelation as a pastoral letter. The book is addressed to "the seven churches that are in Asia" (v 4), and they are specifically named in verse 11. But why seven churches? Why not one? In ancient times, the number seven symbolized wholeness or completion. Apparently, John wants us to see the unity of the church amid its diversity, as well as its diversity in unity. Each local church contains part of the truth that the Lord expects the church to proclaim, and each has a portion of the gospel light. Only when they work together can the full-orbed beauty of the gospel be seen.

Each of the seven churches is experiencing difficulty and hardship of some kind. This perhaps explains why God's messenger declares to them seven encouraging truths about Jesus Christ, the one "who is and who was and who is to come" (v 4).

In verse 5, he explains that Jesus *is the faithful witness* (Gk. *martyr*). Jesus bore witness to the truth not only with his words but especially with his life—and death. He *is the firstborn of the dead*. Jesus conquered death. Therefore, he holds the keys. He *is the ruler of kings on earth*. Jesus *is* King of kings and Lord of lords—forever. And he *is the one who loves us*. Note the present tense. Jesus' love has always been a continuing reality.

The remainder of verses 5 and 6 tells us what Jesus *has done*. He *has freed us* from our sins by his blood. The book of Revelation introduces us to the Lamb who was slain. He *has consecrated us* as a kingdom of priests. In other words, the church is to be to the current world what the Levitical priests were to Israel: mediators and intercessors with God.

Finally, verse 7 tells us what Jesus *will do* in the future. He *is coming again*. He will return with all authority and power, this time riding on a white stallion, not a donkey (see 19:11).

As if to confirm this powerful declaration by his angel, God says, "I am the Alpha and Omega…who is and who was and who is to come, the Almighty" (v 8). He is the "A" and the "Z" and all that is in between. He is not constrained by any limitations of time. He is the Eternal Now.

The Vision Begins

Verses 9–11 describe the setting for the revelation that John has received. In the Greek text, the preposition *en* (meanings include *in, within, on, at, by, among*) appears seven times in this passage as John identifies himself to the churches as "your brother and partner" *EN* the tribulation, *EN* (understood) the kingdom, *EN* (understood) patient endurance, and *EN* Jesus. John was also *EN* the island of Patmos "on account of the word of God and the testimony of Jesus" (v 9). Patmos was a hard-labor prison camp. And he was *EN* the Spirit *EN* the Lord's Day. It appears that Christians already made a distinction between the *Sabbath*, the traditional Jewish day of worship, and *the Lord's Day*, the Christian day of worship.

Then John describes two unforgettable images in verses 12–20:

- *Seven Golden Lampstands.* These lampstands represent the seven churches that will receive his book (1:20). The church is not the gospel light itself, but it is meant to carry the light. These churches were plagued with problems: Ephesus had left her first love; Pergamum was dabbling in heresy; Thyatira was tolerating "that woman Jezebel" (2:20); Sardis had a good reputation but was really dead; and Laodicea was spiritually lukewarm. And yet John sees Jesus in the midst of these churches! Even sinful and dysfunctional churches have the capacity to reveal Christ to the world.

- *One Like a Son of Man.* In the Gospels, Jesus refers to himself as the "Son of Man" more than any other title. This expression comes from another apocalyptic book, Daniel:

> *I saw in the night visions, and behold, with the clouds of heaven there came one like a son of man, and he came to the Ancient of Days and was presented before him. And to him was given dominion and glory and a kingdom, that all peoples, nations, and languages should serve him; his dominion is an everlasting dominion, which shall not pass away, and his kingdom one that shall not be destroyed. (Dan 7:13–14)*

John's readers would have understood that this title referred to someone who was divine in his identity and omnipotent in his sovereignty. Jesus Christ fits both descriptions. The one John sees is "clothed with a long robe and with a golden sash around his chest" (Rev 1:13). The Greek word for "robe" is also used in the Septuagint to describe the robe Aaron wore as the great High Priest (see Ex 28:4). Thus, the Son of Man is not only a king but also a priest, and he is exercising both of those responsibilities now!

John then describes seven physical characteristics of the Son of Man:

1. His hair is as white as snow (see v 14), because he is both wise and pure.
2. His eyes are like a flame of fire (see v 14), of penetrating intensity. Christ looks not only *at* us but also *into* us.
3. His feet are "like burnished bronze" (v 15), indicating that he will stand forever, unlike Daniel's vision of a statue representing a temporal, earthly kingdom, whose feet were "partly of iron and partly of clay" (Dan 2:33).

4. His voice is like "the roar of many waters" (v 15). No human heard the word by which God spoke the universe into being (see John 1:1–18), and when Jesus was on the earth, most failed to hear what he said. But when Christ returns, everyone on the earth will hear what the Son of Man has to say.

5. His right hand holds seven stars (see v 16). Many in the ancient world believed their fate was controlled by the stars just as many today believe in astrology. But it is Jesus who controls the stars. He is not controlled by them!

6. His mouth wields a "sharp two-edged sword" (v 16), which represents the Word of God, the Son of Man's only weapon (see 2:12, 16; 19:15, 21; Heb 4:12; Eph 6:17). His Word penetrates and discerns our deepest thoughts and intentions.

7. His face is like the sun shining at midday (see v 16). Perhaps John was reminded of seeing Jesus on the Mount of Transfiguration, where the Lord's face "shone like the sun" (Matt 17:2).

Confronted by such a striking vision of the Son of Man, John pays close attention to what the Lord says personally to him in verses 17–19.

- *"Fear not."* Although John's vision is unlike anything any human being has ever seen, he has no reason to fear because he is already in the Kingdom (see vv 9–10). Jacques Ellul says that the entire book of Revelation "can be summed up in this word: *fear not.*"[5]

- *"I have the keys of Death and Hades."* What the Lord shuts, no one can open. What he opens, no one can shut. Nothing of eternal consequence happens without the permission of King Jesus.

- *"Write therefore."* Other believers need to know the vision John has seen and hear the words he has heard. He records them in the book of Revelation for all posterity.

---

5 Jacques Ellul, *Apocalypse: The Book of Revelation* (New York: Seabury Press, 1977), 105.

The Excellency of Christ

We have noted that this book is "the revelation of Jesus Christ" (1:1), and already in John's first chapter we have seen both who Jesus is and what Jesus has done and will do. Jonathan Edwards (1703–58) preached a famous sermon entitled, "The Excellency of Christ," and spoke of the fact that the final revelation of Jesus Christ shows him to be both a Lamb and a Lion, not one *or* the other but *both*—at the same time! His text was Revelation 5:5–6, perhaps the most poignant description of this double-reality of Jesus Christ:

> *And one of the elders said to me, "Weep no more; behold, the **Lion** of the tribe of Judah, the Root of David, has conquered, so that he can open the scroll and its seven seals." And between the throne and the four living creatures and among the elders I saw a **Lamb** standing, as though it had been slain. (Emphasis added)*

The purpose of Edwards' sermon was to show the "admirable conjunction of diverse excellencies in Jesus Christ." His lengthy sermon (35 pages) shows the contrasting admirable qualities that meet in the person and in the work of Jesus:

As the Lamb, Jesus is...	As the Lion, Jesus is...
Infinite in condescension	Infinite in exaltation
Infinite in grace	Infinite in justice
Infinite in humility	Infinite in glory
Infinite in meekness	Infinite in majesty
Infinite in submission	Infinite in dominion
Fully reliant on God	Self-sufficient
The sacrifice for our sin	The judge of our sin
Delivered to his enemies	Victorious over his enemies

At his first coming, Jesus came humbly, riding on a *donkey*. But when he comes again, he will come on a *white horse* prepared for war (see Rev 19:11–16). And yet these are not two Jesuses but one. Jesus is one divine Person, not two. Behold, the excellency of Jesus Christ!

There's more. As we follow Jesus the Lion/Lamb and allow his Spirit to transform our hearts and lives, we begin to reflect his glory and discover that his image is *recreated in us*! When we are in Christ, we, too, become lamb-like and lion-like *at the same time*.

> *And we all, with unveiled face, beholding the glory of the Lord, are being transformed into the same image from one degree of glory to another. For this comes from the Lord who is the Spirit. (2 Cor 3:18)*

Living in the Time In-Between

We live today in the time period between the two comings of Christ. He came as a Lamb the first time, and many did not recognize him. When he comes again, he will come as a Lion, and everyone will know his true identity. But you may wonder: Why this interval? Why wouldn't Christ come to us initially in all his power and glory so that no one would mistake who he is? Why will he wait until his return to make his identity crystal clear to everyone when salvation will no longer be possible? C. S. Lewis speaks eloquently to this question in his book, *Mere Christianity*:

> *I wonder whether people who ask God to interfere openly and directly in our world quite realize what it will be like when He does. When that happens, it is the end of the world. When the author walks on to the stage the play is over. God is going to invade, all right: but what is the good of saying you are on His side then, when you see the whole natural universe melting away like a dream and something else—something it never entered your head to conceive—comes crashing in; something so beautiful to some of us and so terrible to others that none of us*

will have any choice left? For this time it will be God without disguise, something so overwhelming that it will strike either irresistible love or irresistible horror into every creature. It will be too late then to choose your side.... That will not be the time for choosing: it will be the time when we discover which side we really have chosen.... Now, today, this moment, is our chance to choose the right side. God is holding back to give us that chance. It will not last forever. We must take it or leave it.[6]

For Reflection and Discussion

1. Explain what it means for you personally to live in the time "in-between," that time period between Christ's first and second comings, between the promise and the fulfillment, the "already" and the "not yet."

2. What difference does it make in our daily lives to realize that Jesus Christ is eternal and lives in the "eternal now," not subject to the laws of past, present, and future?

3. John saw Christ "in the midst" (1:13) of the lampstands representing Asia's dysfunctional churches. Do you believe it is possible to find Christ outside of the church? Explain your answer.

4. When you think of Jesus, which image more readily comes to mind, the Lamb or the Lion? Does the thought of him make you feel secure or does it inspire fear?

---

6 C. S. Lewis, *Mere Christianity* (New York: Macmillan, 1956), 64–65.

2.
Letters to Seven Churches
(Rev 2:1–3:22)

A map of the New Testament world shows us that the churches addressed in the book of Revelation were all located in Asia Minor (today, Turkey) and formed a kind of preaching circuit. John apparently intended that his book would be read as a circular letter by the churches for which he had a measure of pastoral responsibility. It is important to note, however, that none of these churches exists today. How should we understand this historical fact? Can a body of believers born of God cease to live? Can Christians fall from grace? Can a church's lampstand be removed? Let's find out.

I love to visit churches. As a pastor, I find it to be a highly educational activity. The liturgy (or lack of it), the building, the people, the music, and the hospitality all give an indication of what kind of church it is. Looking more closely, I might examine the demographics of the congregation: Rich or poor? White or black? Young or old? I would perhaps take my cue from their style of worship (traditional, contemporary, etc.) to determine whether or not I stayed. I might read their doctrinal statement or check out the amount of money they give to missions. A look in the nursery might give me a clue to their attitude toward children. All of us have such criteria that we use to help us to ascertain whether a church is healthy or dysfunctional, orthodox or heretical, good or bad. Whether consciously or subconsciously, we all have our methods for evaluating a church. But the question that really matters is this: What criteria does Jesus use to measure a church? How does Jesus determine whether a church is right or wrong?

In chapters 2 and 3 of Revelation, Christ is personally making an on-site inspection of seven different churches: observing, warning, commending, rebuking, and encouraging them. What criteria does Jesus use when he looks at the church? How does he measure the health of a congregation? What categories does he use to determine whether a church is good or bad? The answer to these questions becomes clear in the pastoral letters to the seven churches of Asia.

Though each letter is worthy of separate study, the real message contained in these letters is found in viewing them all together. The letters are the means through which the Spirit of God addresses a message not just to one church but to them all. "He who has an ear, let him hear what the Spirit says to the *churches*" (see 2:7, 11, 17, 29; 3:6, 13, 22, emphasis added). The message of Revelation is not just one message for one church in one age. Rather, the entire church needs to hear what Christ has to say to all seven congregations, and this is true whether we are living in first-century Rome or twenty-first-century America. Let's take a look, then, at each of these churches, asking the Lord of the church to help us see ourselves and our own congregations through the lens of these historic assemblies.

Ephesus: The Loveless Church (Rev 2:1–7)

Ephesus was the third largest city of the Roman Empire. It was a very important commercial center, boasting a population of over 250,000 people. Three great trade routes converged on this city. It had an impressive marketplace, a theater, and a large stadium that seated some 25,000 spectators. The dominant feature of its skyline was the magnificent temple built on the mountain above the city in honor of the goddess Diana (or Artemis). It was four times larger than the Parthenon in Athens and is still widely regarded as one of the Seven Wonders of the Ancient World.

On his third missionary journey, the apostle Paul spent three years in this city, preaching and teaching, first in the synagogue and then in the lecture hall of Tyrannus. In fact, Paul spent more time in this city than any other city in which he ministered.

The ministry in Ephesus was so successful that the church became a missionary church, and through its ministry "all the residents of Asia heard the word of the Lord, both Jews and Greeks" (Acts 19:10). In other words, Ephesus was the mother church for the other six churches of Asia mentioned in Revelation 2–3.

But it was not all smooth sailing. Acts 19 tells about a huge riot that broke out in the city, instigated by a silversmith named Demetrius. He was upset because Paul's preaching was having an adverse effect on the local economy. Sales on little silver idols of Diana were plummeting. So Demetrius instigated a riot that almost brought Paul to a violent end.

Acts 20:17–38 is a beautiful and tender picture of Paul's final meeting with the elders of the church at Ephesus on the island of Miletus. In this passage, the apostle gave final instructions to the leaders of the church, encouraging them to stand strong and warning them of dangers to come:

Pay careful attention to yourselves and to all the flock, in which the Holy Spirit has made you overseers, to care for the church of God, which he obtained with his own blood. I know that after my departure fierce wolves will come in among you, not sparing the flock; and from among your own selves will arise men speaking twisted things, to draw away the disciples after them. Therefore be alert.... (Acts 20:28–31)

One of the pastors who followed Paul at Ephesus was young Timothy. Paul seems to have put him in charge of the work, and the epistle of 1 Timothy was likely written to encourage him in his responsibilities (see 1 Tim 1:3). Tradition indicates that the apostle John (the one writing the book of Revelation) also pastored this church. He may well have been a bishop, giving oversight not only to Ephesus but to the surrounding daughter churches as well. It is possible that the letter of 1 John was written primarily to the church at Ephesus but circulated to the others as well. Many believe that John made Ephesus his home, living there for many years, taking care of Mary, the mother of Jesus (see John 19:26–27).

Yes, Ephesus was an impressive church. Imagine having Paul as your first pastor, followed by Timothy and John! And imagine that the mother of Jesus was sitting on the second pew each Sunday morning! Imagine that several books of the New Testament were addressed to your congregation! This church was immensely blessed. Little wonder that when Jesus wrote to this church, he had many positive things to say:

> *I know your works, your toil and your patient endurance, and how you cannot bear with those who are evil, but have tested those who call themselves apostles and are not, and found them to be false. I know you are enduring patiently and bearing up for my name's sake, and you have not grown weary. (Rev 2:2–3)*

The Ephesians were active in their service to God and their ministry to one another. They stood steady in adversity. They remained orthodox in their theology, not only detecting error but also having the courage to expose it and bring church discipline to bear upon it.

Yet in spite of these remarkable qualities, the one who has eyes "like a flame of fire" (1:14) has a criticism. Only one defect in the church is noted, but it is something that affects everything else: "You have abandoned the love you had at first" (2:4). In other words, they were doing the right things but *for the wrong reasons.* Jesus had warned his disciples of the danger of this happening. "Because lawlessness will be increased, the love of many will grow cold" (Matt 24:12). In the believers at Ephesus we see the sad results. Acts of worship and deeds of kindness that were once done spontaneously and joyfully out of passionate love for Jesus were now done out of habit, routine, or even duty. They were doing what was right, but their hearts were no longer in it! Lovelessness is like a spiritual cancer, and Jesus warned, "Remember therefore from where you have fallen; repent, and do the works you did at first. If not, I will come to you and remove your lampstand from its place, unless you repent" (Rev 2:5).

Only one thing is wrong with the Ephesian church, just one: their good works are no longer motivated by love. And because of this, the Lord of the church is threatening to remove their lampstand and let them cease to exist! Thankfully, Jesus not only exposes the problem but also points to a solution. They must *remember* the relationship they once had with God, *repent* (i.e., turn away) from the routine way they are doing things, and *return* to the passionate devotion they once had for God. Without genuine love for God, our faith is nothing. Paul said he might speak in the tongues of angels, have the gift of prophecy, exercise impressive faith, and even give his body to be burned as a martyr, but if he wasn't motivated by love, it meant nothing at all (see 1 Cor 13:1–3).

Be sure to notice verse 7: "To the one who conquers, I will grant to eat of the tree of life, which is in the paradise of God." Even if a congregation is characterized by lovelessness and operating on spiritual autopilot, individual members don't have to be this way. In other words, your church may be cold and frozen, but *you* don't have to be!

Ephesus at a Glance

Historical Context	• Acts 19:1–41; 20:17–38 and the book of Ephesians • Heresy and pseudo-apostles • Persecution
Titles of Christ	The one "who holds the seven stars in his right hand, who walks among the seven golden lampstands" (Rev 2:1)

Commendations	"I know your works, your toil and your patient endurance, and how you cannot bear with those who are evil, but have tested those who call themselves apostles and are not, and found them to be false. I know you are enduring patiently and bearing up for my name's sake, and you have not grown weary" (Rev 2:2–3).
Rebukes	"But I have this against you, that you have abandoned the love you had at first" (Rev 2:4).
Commands	"Remember therefore from where you have fallen; repent, and do the works you did at first" (Rev 2:5).
Warnings	"If not, I will come to you and remove your lampstand from its place, unless you repent" (Rev 2:5).
Promises	"To the one who conquers I will grant to eat of the tree of life, which is in the paradise of God" (Rev 2:7).
Major Theme	Without love, our faith is nothing.
Message for Us	Do the right things for the right reasons.

Smyrna: The Persecuted Church (Rev 2:8–11)

The church at Ephesus taught us that the first mark of a true church is love. The church at Smyrna teaches us that a second mark is suffering. One trait leads to the next. A church that loves is a church that suffers. Although all seven of the churches were undergoing some form of persecution, Smyrna seemed to experience the worst.

In the first century, Smyrna was one of the most beautiful cities in Asia, prosperous and rich in history. The city had been planned and rebuilt by Alexander the Great. Homer, author of the *Odyssey*, once lived there. The city had very close ties to Rome. In fact, Smyrna held Rome in such high esteem that she was the first city to build a temple to the Roman spirit and the goddess Roma in 195 bc. By the time this letter was written, Smyrna was one of the strongest centers of emperor worship in all the Roman Empire. This single fact helps to explain much of the persecution the Smyrnan church endured.

Among the seven churches, only two have nothing negative said about them: Smyrna (see 2:8–11) and Philadelphia (see 3:7–13). It's surely no coincidence that the church that needed no correction was a church undergoing persecution. Persecution tends to purify the church.

It is possible that when this letter was read to the church in Smyrna near the end of the first century, the pastor was a young man named Polycarp. John wrote the book of Revelation around AD 90–95, and we know that by AD 110 Polycarp had become bishop of Smyrna, where he served for several decades. He was widely respected and loved in that area of the world, a beloved pastor and a strong voice for orthodox theology.

Polycarp was perhaps the most famous martyr of the second century. We even know the date: February 23 of AD 155, and Polycarp was in his eighties. When the soldiers came to arrest him, he welcomed them as if they were his friends, providing a meal and making sure their needs were met. He asked only for an extra hour to pray before they took him away.

But as the soldiers listened to him pray, they began to second-guess their mission: What was so dangerous about this old, saintly pastor? Why did he need to be killed?

As they led him into the city, the captain of the guard pled with Polycarp to say the magic words so he would not be killed. "What harm is there in saying *Caesar is Lord* and offering a pinch of incense as a sacrifice to the emperor?" he asked. But Polycarp would not compromise. He knew there was only one Lord, and his name was *not* Caesar!

This is the shortest of the letters to the seven churches, but its content is rich. Christ is writing to a persecuted church, and he begins by stating three things he knows about them. First, he says, "I know your tribulation" (v 9). The Greek word literally means "pressure," and it refers to external forces that threaten to crush the Christian faith right out of them. Roman law said citizens must offer incense in worship to Caesar. Believers in this city were living in a pressure cooker.

Second, Jesus says, he knows their poverty. Two Greek words are translated "poverty" in the New Testament. One word refers to a person who has a bare subsistence, just enough resources to get by. The other word refers to someone who has nothing at all. It is the second word that is used here. The believers of Smyrna lived in abject poverty, doubtless because of the persecution they were suffering. Perhaps their homes and businesses had been destroyed. Perhaps they had been confined to a ghetto, like those of the Jews in Poland and Germany during World War II. Perhaps they refused to give or take bribes and participate in the corrupt practices of tax collectors and dishonest businessmen. Perhaps their children were refused jobs or entrance into the cities' schools.

Third, Jesus knows about the slander they are experiencing. The word *slander* literally means "blasphemy." They were being maligned, discredited, and defamed. Slander is one of Satan's most effective weapons against believers. He seeks to undermine our witness for Christ by spreading lies, rumors, and gossip about us. This was the experience of Christians in Smyrna, and Jesus knew it.

After acknowledging their suffering and difficult circumstances, Jesus then tells these believers how to weather the storm of persecution. He does not advise them to pray that the storm won't hit, because *it already has*! Rather, Jesus exhorts this little flock not to be afraid. They must "be faithful unto death" (2:10). In the end, God's victorious saints will be those who "loved not their lives even unto death" (12:11). They will wear crowns of life (see 2:10) and "will not be hurt by the second death" (2:11).

In our own time, many seem blissfully unaware that storm clouds of persecution against the church are gathering. But we should not be surprised by opposition and suffering. The New Testament frequently reminds us that this is to be our lot as Christians:

- 1 Pet 4:12–13—"Beloved, do not be surprised at the fiery trial when it comes upon you to test you, as though something strange were happening to you. But rejoice insofar as you share Christ's sufferings, that you may also rejoice and be glad when his glory is revealed."

- Acts 14:22—"Through many tribulations we must enter the kingdom of God."

- Luke 6:26—"Woe to you, when all people speak well of you, for so their fathers did to the false prophets."

- Mark 13:12–13—"Brother will deliver brother over to death, and the father his child, and children will rise against parents and have them put to death. And you will be hated by all for my name's sake. But the one who endures to the end will be saved."

- John 15:18–20—"If the world hates you, know that it has hated me before it hated you. If you were of the world, the world would love you as its own; but because you are not of the world, but I chose you out of the world, therefore the world hates you. Remember the word that I said to you: 'A servant is not greater than his master.' If

they persecuted me, they will also persecute you. If they kept my word, they will also keep yours."

- 2 Timothy 3:12—"Indeed, all who desire to live a godly life in Christ Jesus will be persecuted."

Smyrna at a Glance

Historical Context	• Persecution • Poverty • Demonic activity
Titles of Christ	"The words of the first and the last, who died and came to life" (Rev 2:8).
Commendations	"I know your tribulation and your poverty (but you are rich) and the slander of those who say that they are Jews and are not, but are a synagogue of Satan" (Rev 2:9).
Rebukes	None. Suffering and persecution tend to purify the church!
Commands	"Do not fear what you are about to suffer…. Be faithful unto death…" (Rev 2:10).
Warnings	None
Promises	"Be faithful unto death, and I will give you the crown of life…. The one who conquers will not be hurt by the second death" (Rev 2:10–11).
Major Theme	Faithfulness in the midst of persecution
Message for Us	God knows our suffering, and he will reward our faithfulness.

Pergamum: The Heretical Church (Rev 2:12–17)

Pergamum was the capital city of the province of Asia, the seat of the Roman government. As a result, it was very influential. It was famous for its library, the second largest in the ancient world (after Alexandria), with some 200,000 volumes. Mark Antony is said to have given the library to Cleopatra for a wedding present. Pergamum was also famous for its temples to the pagan gods. It had temples to Zeus, Athena, Dionysus, and Asklepios (the god of healing, whose symbol was a serpent). In some ways it was like Lourdes, France: thousands of pilgrims went there, hoping to be healed.

But the most important characteristic of this city, at least as far as the church was concerned, was that it was the official center for the imperial cult, emperor worship. Of all the seven cities of Asia, Pergamum was the one in which the church was most likely to clash with the Roman authorities. This is probably why the risen Christ says to the church, "I know where you dwell, where Satan's throne is" (v 13).

Jesus commends the church by recognizing how she has held fast and remained faithful in spite of great adversity: "You hold fast my name, and you did not deny my faith even in the days of Antipas my faithful witness, who was killed among you, where Satan dwells" (2:13). Yet the Lord has something against them: they have allowed false doctrines to creep into the church.

Truth is essential to the Christian life. Twice in this letter, Jesus is described as having a sword—a sharp, two-edged sword coming out of his mouth (see vv 12, 16). He is similarly described in Revelation 1:16 and 19:15, 21. On at least two other occasions in the New Testament, a sword in used to symbolize the Word of God (see Eph 6:17; Heb 4:12–13). Similarly, here in Revelation, the sword that comes out of Christ's mouth represents the decisive truth of both who he is and what he says. Jesus not only *speaks* the truth; he *is* the truth (see John 14:6).

Perhaps you've heard the story of the old Jewish rabbi who was holding court in his village. Two women, who were in an argument, came to the rabbi to decide the case. After the first woman spoke, the rabbi said, "You are right." Then the second woman spoke and gave a totally opposite description of what had happened. "You are right," said the rabbi. The rabbi's wife was present and so she blurted out, "You stupid old man, they can't both be right," to which the rabbi replied, "You are right too."

This is the kind of world we live in today. We say, "I have my truths and you have your truths. Yes, our opinions may be mutually contradictory, but let's not worry about a minor detail like that! Let's just pretend we're all right." The risen Christ leaves no room for such relativism. Some things are true and some things are false. Jesus has zero tolerance for false beliefs in his church.

The church at Pergamum considered itself to be tolerant and broad-minded. These folks were not judgmental—just the opposite! They were sophisticated, open-minded people who would be hesitant to call anyone a heretic. It is unlikely that everyone in the Pergamum church believed false doctrines and practiced perverted lifestyles, but they said nothing to oppose those who did. This is why the risen Christ arrives with a sharp sword coming out of his mouth. He comes to cut through the fog of relativism and moral ambiguity and lay bare the truth of God before the eyes of this wayward church.

> But I have a few things against you: you have some there who hold the teaching of Balaam, who taught Balak to put a stumbling block before the sons of Israel, so that they might eat food sacrificed to idols and practice sexual immorality. So also you have some who hold the teaching of the Nicolaitans. (vv 14–15)

The heresy in Pergamum involved idolatry and sexual immorality. The reference to "the teaching of Balaam" refers to the incident in the Old Testament where this false prophet instigated a plan for Moabite women to seduce Hebrew men (see Num 25:1–18, 31:15–16). The Nicolaitans seem to have been a sect that taught that Christians were no longer accountable to the moral law. They thought they could eat and drink as they pleased, treat the Sabbath as just another day, engage in sexual promiscuity, and live in greedy materialism—and still be followers of Jesus Christ! Jesus wanted this church to know that such moral and theological relativism would not be tolerated in his church!

The real proof of our doctrine is our behavior and our character. Bad behavior proves that false doctrines are present. The only solution is to repent of our waywardness and turn back to the one who has a sword coming out of his mouth! That was the Lord's command to Pergamum, and it applies to us as well. The truth may not make us feel better, at least not at first, because it is a sword. It cuts. It hurts. It exposes what is rotten. But like a surgeon's scalpel, the truth eventually makes healing possible.

Pergamum at a Glance

Historical Context	• Emperor worship • Antipas had been martyred for his faith
Titles of Christ	"The words of him who has the sharp two-edged sword" (Rev 2:12).
Commendations	"I know where you dwell, where Satan's throne is. Yet you hold fast my name, and you did not deny my faith even in the days of Antipas my faithful witness, who was killed among you, where Satan dwells" (Rev 2:13).
Rebukes	"But I have a few things against you: you have some there who hold the teaching of Balaam, who taught Balak to put a stumbling block before the sons of Israel, so that they might eat food sacrificed to idols and practice sexual immorality. So also you have some who hold the teaching of the Nicolaitans" (Rev 2:14–15).
Commands	"Therefore repent" (Rev 2:16).

Warnings	"If not, I will come to you soon and war against them with the sword of my mouth" (Rev 2:16).
Promises	"To the one who conquers I will give some of the hidden manna, and I will give him a white stone, with a new name written on the stone that no one knows except the one who receives it" (Rev 2:17).
Major Theme	Doctrinal error and immorality
Message for Us	The sharp, two-edged sword in Jesus' mouth either exposes our hearts and saves us (like a surgeon's scalpel) or destroys us (like an enemy's weapon).

Thyatira: The Tolerant Church (Rev 2:18–29)

Ironically, the longest of the seven letters is written to the church in the smallest city. We really don't know much about the city of Thyatira except that it was a commercial center that excelled in woolen fabric dyed the color purple. One of Thyatira's businesswomen, Lydia, ended up in Philippi and there met the apostle Paul (see Acts 16:14). She became the first Christian convert in Europe.

The Lord commends the church at Thyatira for her deeds, her love, her faith, her service, and her endurance. Especially noteworthy is the fact that her "latter works exceed the first" (2:19). In other words, this was a loving, vibrant church, growing in both depth and breadth. Yet something was wrong. "You tolerate that woman Jezebel, who calls herself a prophetess and is teaching and seducing my servants to practice sexual immorality and to eat food sacrificed to idols" (2:20).

Thyatira makes an interesting contrast to Ephesus. Ephesus was orthodox in its teaching but cold in its practice. She had abandoned the love she had at first (see 2:4). Thyatira, on the other hand, was warm in its fellowship but theologically confused. She tolerated that woman Jezebel (see 2:20). At the risk of oversimplification, we could say that Ephesus had truth without love; Thyatira had love without truth. Which church would you rather attend? The tragic reality is that many Christians today must choose between these two options as they look for a home church.

Some will choose a church like Thyatira, saying, "I really like *that* church because the people are so nice and you can so easily feel connected. The pastor is warm and nurturing; his sermons make me feel so good. Yeah, sometimes his teachings are a little bizarre and he veers far astray from the Bible, but that's OK, I suppose. It's all about love, right?" Others will prefer a church like Ephesus, saying, "I really like *that* church because they preach the truth. They take Bible doctrine seriously, and I actually learn something when I go there. No one seems to know one another and

it feels like a lecture hall, but that's OK, I suppose. It's all about the truth, right?"

John wants his readers to understand that the church of Jesus Christ must be a place where truth and love dwell *together* in all of their confrontational splendor. Paul understood the importance of this when he wrote about the need to speak "the truth in love" so that we are able "to grow up in every way into him who is the head, into Christ" (Eph 4:15).

Whether there existed an actual woman with the literal name Jezebel in the city of Thyatira is open to debate. Probably, John was referring to a real woman in the congregation whose influence was similar to that of the wicked Queen Jezebel in Israel one thousand years earlier (see 2 Kings 9). Queen Jezebel had led God's people astray by introducing other gods and encouraging sexual immorality. Apparently, a prophetess in Thyatira was teaching a doctrine similar to that of the Nicolaitans and the followers of Balaam that we saw earlier in Pergamum. Moreover, this seductive woman was teaching people the "deep things of Satan" (v 24). This may have been an early form of Gnosticism.

Note it well that the real problem in Thyatira was neither Jezebel nor those who followed her and her evil teachings. God would take care of them personally (see vv 22–23). The real problem was that the church *tolerated* this evil woman and her evil teachings (see v 20). Apparently, many in the church were too discerning to be sucked into her seductive ways themselves, but they passively permitted her influence to remain in the church. They did nothing to stop her.

Today in western culture, tolerance is perhaps the cardinal virtue of our society. We hear the importance of tolerance preached from our public schools, media, entertainment industry, and government. We pride ourselves on how open we are to everyone. No one has stated this reality more eloquently than Allan Bloom in his influential book *The Closing of the American Mind,* written in 1987:

There is one thing a professor can be absolutely certain of: almost every student entering the university believes, or says he believes, that truth is relative.... Some are religious, some atheists; some are to the Left, some to the Right; some intend to be scientists, some humanists or professionals or businessmen; some are poor, some rich. They are unified only in their relativism and in their allegiance to equality.... The relativity of truth is not a theoretical insight but a moral postulate, the condition of a free society, or so they see it.... The danger they have been taught to fear from absolutism is not error but intolerance. Relativism is necessary to openness; and this is the virtue, the only virtue, which all primary education for more than fifty years has dedicated itself to inculcating.... The true believer is the real danger. The study of history and of culture teaches that all the world was mad in the past; men always thought they were right, and that led to wars, persecutions, slavery, xenophobia, racism, and chauvinism. The point is not to correct the mistakes and really be right; rather it is not to think you are right at all.[7]

Part of the problem here is that our definition of *tolerance* has changed dramatically. Traditionally, tolerance simply meant the commitment to recognize and respect another person's beliefs and practices, without necessarily agreeing with them. But that is not what our culture means by tolerance today. Today's definition is not about respecting those with whom we differ but rather about the philosophical proposition that all beliefs and all lifestyles are equally valid. The new tolerance does not simply allow others to have their own opinions. No, the new tolerance demands that I accept them, support them, and to some extent agree with them.

Perhaps the best-loved verse in the Bible today is Matthew 7:1—"Judge not, that you be not judged." No verse is quoted more often when someone is exalting the virtues of tolerance. But let's look at this verse in its broader context:

---

7 Allan Bloom, *The Closing of the American Mind* (New York: Simon and Schuster, 1987), 25–26.

*Judge not, that you be not judged. For with the judgment you pro-
nounce you will be judged, and with the measure you use it will be
measured to you. Why do you see the speck that is in your brother's eye,
but do not notice the log that is in your own eye? Or how can you say to
your brother, 'Let me take the speck out of your eye,' when there is the
log in your own eye? You hypocrite, first take the log out of your own
eye, and then you will see clearly to take the speck out of your brother's eye. Do not give dogs what is holy, and do not throw your pearls
before pigs, lest they trample them underfoot and turn to attack you.
(Matt 7:1–6)*

Jesus is not telling us to avoid making distinctions or discriminating
between what is true or false, good or bad. To the contrary! He is warning
us not to judge others hypocritically, self-righteously, or harshly in a spirit
of condescending superiority. In fact, he wants us to take the log out of
our own eye *so that* we can see clearly to help our brother with the speck
in his. Why would he tell us not to give holy and precious things to "dogs"
or "swine" unless he expected us to discriminate between people's spiritual
sincerity?

Christians today face no greater challenge than learning how to live
their faith in a pluralistic, relativistic, multicultural society. The same challenge faced Christians in the first century living in the city of Thyatira.
Unfortunately, they chose to do nothing about the falsehood that confronted them, even within the church itself. Hopefully, believers today will
respond with more wisdom and courage than they did in the church at
Thyatira. Peter offers counsel to Christians seeking help in responding to
the ungodly beliefs and lifestyles all around them:

*But in your hearts honor Christ the Lord as holy, always being prepared
to make a defense to anyone who asks you for a reason for the hope
that is in you; yet do it with gentleness and respect, having a good conscience, so that, when you are slandered, those who revile your good
behavior in Christ may be put to shame. (1 Pet 3:15–16)*

Historical Context	A prophetess (Jezebel) has a huge influence in the city and is seducing followers of Christ to practice sexual immorality and eat food sacrificed to idols.
Titles of Christ	"The words of the Son of God, who has eyes like a flame of fire, and whose feet are like burnished bronze....I am he who searches mind and heart, and I will give to each of you according to your works" (Rev 2:18, 23).
Commendations	"I know your works, your love and faith and service and patient endurance, and that your latter works exceed the first" (Rev 2:19).
Rebukes	"But I have this against you, that you tolerate that woman Jezebel" (Rev 2:20).
Commands	"Only hold fast what you have until I come" (Rev 2:25).
Warnings	"Behold, I will throw her onto a sickbed, and those who commit adultery with her I will throw into great tribulation, unless they repent of her works, 23 and I will strike her children dead" (Rev 2:22–23).
Promises	"The one who conquers and who keeps my works until the end, to him I will give authority over the nations....And I will give him the morning star" (Rev 2:26, 28).
Major Theme	God will not tolerate false teaching in the church.
Message for Us	Christians must not remain silent when God's people practice sexual immorality and promote doctrines that are false.

Sardis: The Deceived Church (Rev 3:1–6)

An oxymoron is the occurrence of two words together that normally are mutually contradictory. Humorous examples include "jumbo shrimp," "pretty ugly," or "ill health." While many oxymorons are funny, what we find in the city of Sardis is not funny at all: a *dead church*. How is that possible? By definition, a church is alive. After all, it is composed of members of the body of Christ, men and women who have been given new life by the Spirit of the living God. How can a church, which is so intimately connected with the living God, be dead? And yet the church at Sardis, though only about fifty years old, was already spiritually dead. That verdict didn't come from a disgruntled church member or a discouraged pastor; no, the pronouncement of death came from the lips of Christ himself: "You have the reputation of being alive, but you are dead" (3:1).

There was no hint of heresy in the church at Sardis. As far as we can tell by the New Testament account, it was orthodox in its teachings. But the Lord had nothing good to say about this congregation, other than the fact that a few of its members had not "soiled their garments" (3:4). All of the spiritual vitality had drained out of it. But don't assume the church was empty or inactive. To the contrary, Sardis was probably as busy as the other congregations mentioned in Revelation 2–3. Indeed, she had a reputation for being alive. As far as her neighbors were concerned, this was a lively place. But as the saying goes, you can't judge a book by its cover, nor can you judge a church by its busy calendar.

So how could the church at Sardis know it was dead? That question poses a real problem, because spiritually dead people, by definition, don't know they are spiritually dead. To ask the question in a different manner: How can people who are spiritually deceived—thinking they are alive and right with God when the truth is just the opposite—know they are spiritually deceived? Is there any way to guard against self-deception?

Fortunately, the Bible has a lot to say about this important subject. On at least six occasions in the New Testament, we are warned not to deceive ourselves. These references make it possible to formulate six questions for self-examination to avoid self-deception:

1. *Do I consider myself to be wise?* "Let no one deceive himself. If anyone among you thinks that he is wise in this age, let him become a fool that he may become wise. For the wisdom of this world is folly with God. For it is written, 'He catches the wise in their craftiness'" (1 Cor 3:18–19). Even the pagan philosophers Plato and Aristotle figured this one out. The first mark of wisdom is to recognize and admit what a fool one is.

2. *Is there unconfessed sin in my life?* "Do not be deceived: neither the sexually immoral, nor idolaters, nor adulterers, nor men who practice homosexuality, nor thieves, nor the greedy, nor drunkards, nor revilers, nor swindlers will inherit the kingdom of God" (1 Cor 6:9–10). Jesus came to save us from our sins, not to leave us in them. Those who think they can continue in willful, known, habitual sin and yet call themselves children of God are spiritually deceived.

3. *Do my friends draw me toward Christ or away from him?* "Do not be deceived: 'Bad company ruins good morals'" (1 Cor 15:33). If we hang out with people who have the flu, we should not be surprised when we get sick. Why can't we see the parallels between physical disease and spiritual disease?

4. *Do I think I am immune from the consequences of my sinful choices?* "Do not be deceived: God is not mocked, for whatever one sows, that will he also reap. For the one who sows to his own flesh will from the flesh reap corruption, but the one who sows to the Spirit will from the Spirit reap eternal life" (Gal 6:7–8). Sinners prove their lost condition when they claim their choices will not lead to

tragic consequences—both in this world and in the world to come. If we sow "wild oats," we will reap a harvest of destruction.

5. *Am I doing what God directs me to do in his Word?* "But be doers of the word, and not hearers only, deceiving yourselves" (James 1:22). Tragically, many in evangelical churches have drawn the false conclusion that because they know what the Bible says, they are therefore spiritually right with God. Knowledge of scripture is no substitute for doing what it says.

6. *Do I control my tongue?* "If anyone thinks he is religious and does not bridle his tongue but deceives his heart, this person's religion is worthless" (James 1:26). What comes out of a person's mouth is an infallible indicator of what's on that person's inside. It's no use pretending your motives are pure if your language is filthy.

The members of the church of Sardis were deceived. They thought they were spiritually alive when the truth was they were spiritually dead. Jesus spoke to the church, giving them four commands that—if followed—promised to wake them out of their spiritual turpitude and bring them back to life:

Wake up! Strengthen what remains and is about to die, for I have found your deeds unfinished in the sight of my God. Remember, therefore, what you have received and heard; hold it fast, and repent. But if you do not wake up, I will come like a thief, and you will not know at what time I will come to you. (3:2–3 NIV)

Wake up! This command was especially significant for the people of Sardis, because their city had been captured on two occasions when the guards were asleep. No spiritual sleep is so deep that the voice of Christ is unable to awaken it. Even when Lazarus had been dead for four days, the voice of the Lord calling his name brought him to life (see John 11:43–44).

Remember. If we remember the joy, zeal, and passion we felt for the Lord when we first committed our lives to him, we are less likely to be seduced away from him.

Hold it fast [obey]. We are saved by grace through faith and not by works of obedience, and yet faith without works is dead. One proves the presence of the other. If we love Jesus, we will do what he says.

Repent. The word literally means "to turn, to have a change of mind." Repentance is the key to spiritual life and victory. Self-deception ends the moment we turn from trusting in our own understanding and instead put our confidence in Christ alone.

Sardis at a Glance

Historical Context	There is no indication of persecution from the outside or heresy on the inside.
Titles of Christ	"These are the words of him who holds the seven spirits of God and the seven stars" (Rev 3:1 NIV).
Commendations	"Yet you have a few people in Sardis who have not soiled their clothes. They will walk with me, dressed in white, for they are worthy" (Rev 3:4 NIV).
Rebukes	"I know your deeds; you have a reputation of being alive, but you are dead" (Rev 3:1 NIV).
Commands	"Wake up! Strengthen what remains and is about to die….Remember, therefore, what you have received and heard; hold it fast, and repent" (Rev 3:2–3 NIV).
Warnings	"But if you do not wake up, I will come like a thief, and you will not know at what time I will come to you" (Rev 3:3 NIV).
Promises	"They will walk with me, dressed in white…. I will never blot out the name of that person from the book of life, but will acknowledge that name before my Father and his angels" (Rev 3:4–5 NIV).
Major Theme	Self-deception
Message for Us	Spiritual life can return to us when we wake up, remember, obey, and repent.

Philadelphia: The Missionary Church
(Rev 3:7–13)

Jesus had nothing negative to say about the church in Philadelphia. As with the church at Smyrna, he found no fault with this congregation. "I know that you have but little power," he said (v 8), but it did not seem to be a rebuke or criticism, just a statement of fact. The church was not very large or influential, yet they had done two things worthy of special recognition: "You have kept my word and have not denied my name" (v 8). What word had they kept? In verse 10, the Lord specifically says, "You have kept my word about patient endurance." In other words, they stood firm through persecution and suffering. Moreover, they had "not denied my name" (v 8).

In polite society today, you can mention the name of Buddha, Confucius, Muhammad, or the Dalai Lama, and people will give you a respectful hearing; but if you mention the name of Jesus, people draw back as if you were the carrier of some sort of plague.

If you confess at a fashionable cocktail party that you are plotting to overthrow the government, or that you are a PLO terrorist or a KGB spy, or that you molest porcupines or bite bats' heads off, you will soon attract a buzzing, fascinated, sympathetic circle of listeners. But if you confess that you believe Jesus is the Christ, the Son of the living God, you will find yourself suddenly alone, with a distinct chill in the air.[8]

It takes courage to name the name of Jesus. Jesus' followers in Philadelphia were not ashamed or afraid to name the name of Jesus in the public square. They knew that the name of Jesus is the only name that has power to save (see Acts 4:11–12; Phil 2:9–11). Therefore, Jesus himself commends them for not denying his name.

The Lord told them, "Behold, I have set before you an open door, which no one is able to shut" (v 8). This "door" is apparently not the same

---

8 Peter Kreeft, *Fundamentals of the Faith* (San Francisco: Ignatius Press, 1988), 74.

as the door mentioned in Revelation 3:20, the one we are called to open so Christ can enter our lives. Neither is it the door mentioned in Revelation 4:1–2 that allowed John to see into the very throne room of heaven. It seems that the door Jesus is talking about to the church in Philadelphia is an open opportunity for ministry and service to the world around them. Jesus Christ, who holds the key (see v 7), has opened a door of ministry to this church that will enable them to have an evangelistic impact on their city. Though forces of evil may oppose them, Christ is promising his victorious power as they respond in obedience to the "open door" that is before them.

Philadelphia at a Glance

Historical Context	God has given this church a golden opportunity for ministry and cultural impact. (Rev 3:8—"I have set before you an open door.")
Titles of Christ	"The words of the holy one, the true one, who has the key of David, who opens and no one will shut, who shuts and no one opens" (Rev 3:7).
Commendations	"I know that you have but little power, and yet you have kept my word and have not denied my name....You have kept my word about patient endurance" (Rev 3:8, 10).
Rebukes	None
Commands	"Hold fast what you have, so that no one may seize your crown" (Rev 3:11).
Warnings	None

Promises	"I have set before you an open door, which no one is able to shut....I will make them come and bow down before your feet....I will keep you from the hour of trial that is coming on the whole world.... I am coming soon....I will make him a pillar in the temple of my God...and I will write on him the name of my God, and the name of the city of my God, the new Jerusalem, which comes down from my God out of heaven, and my own new name" (Rev 3:8–12).
Major Theme	Jesus has the power to open doors for ministry opportunities, and he has the power to shut them.
Message for Us	When Christ opens an opportunity for ministry, we must respond in obedient faith, regardless of the cost (cf 1 Cor 16:9).

Laodicea: The Mediocre Church (Rev 3:14–22)

The city of Laodicea was perhaps the wealthiest of the seven cities mentioned in Revelation 2–3. In fact, it was one of the wealthiest cities in the Roman Empire. The city was famous for its wool-making, its banking business, and its medical school, which had developed an eye salve that was widely used.

We don't know much about the church in Laodicea. We have no record of who founded it or when, but this letter indicates that by AD 90 the church was in a spiritual crisis. The fire had gone out. I think it is no coincidence that the most dysfunctional church addressed in Revelation was located in the most prosperous city. It seems that the members of the church were like other inhabitants of the city—healthy, prosperous, and content. The letter contains no hint of heresy or persecution, and yet the Lord says to this church, "I am about to spit you out of my mouth" (v 16 NIV). What was it about this church that so sickened and nauseated the risen Lord?

About six miles from Laodicea was a town called Hierapolis, which was famous for its hot springs. These springs were up on cliffs about 300 feet above the valley floor. The cliffs were about a mile long and encrusted with calcium carbonate. As the hot, mineral-rich water flowed over the cliffs, it cooled and became lukewarm. Because of the calcium carbonate now dissolved into the lukewarm water, the waters took on a certain medicinal quality, serving as an emetic for those who drank. In other words, these waters caused people to vomit.

In a similar manner, the halfhearted spirituality of the Laodiceans made the Lord Jesus sick. Their spiritual mediocrity caused him to feel nauseated. Danish theologian Søren Kierkegaard wrote poignantly about the seriousness of such halfhearted commitment:

> *The greatest danger to Christianity is, I contend, not heresies, hetero-doxies, nor atheists, nor profane secularism—no, but the kind of or-thodoxy which is cordial drivel, mediocrity served up sweet.... In the world of mediocrity in which we live it is assumed that only crackpots, fanatics, and the like should be deplored as offensive, as inspired by Satan, and that the middle way is the right way.... Christ is of an-other mind: mediocrity is the worst offense, the most dangerous kind of demon possession... This kind of religion is nothing but a deception.[9]*

Jesus was telling the church that he prefers a passionate atheist to a lukewarm Christian, a fiery humanist to a halfhearted believer! "Would that you were either cold or hot!" (v 15).

The problem at Laodicea was spiritual mediocrity, lukewarmness, half-hearted devotion to Christ. Such a state of affairs was literally giving Christ a bellyache. But what was the *cause* of the problem? Jesus is the Great Physician and like any good doctor he wants to treat not just the symp-toms but the root cause of the disease. His diagnosis is profoundly simple and simply profound: "For you say, I am rich, I have prospered, and I need nothing, not realizing that you are wretched, pitiable, poor, blind, and na-ked" (v 17). The real issue was not that the Laodiceans were spiritually sick but rather that they *didn't know* they were spiritually sick!

It was this ignorance of their ignorance, this blindness to their blind-ness, this refusal to confess their true condition and spiritual poverty that lay at the root of their nauseating condition. Jesus knew the Laodiceans better than they knew themselves and he was offering them a mirror in which they could see their true condition.

Their problem was spiritual mediocrity and the cause of their problem was willful spiritual blindness: they refused to see the truth about them-selves. So how could they regain their sight? How could they see the truth?

---

9 Charles E. Moore, ed., *Provocations: Spiritual Writings of Kierkegaard* (Farmington, PA: Plough Publishing, 1999), 16–18.

Verses 18–20 outline four prescriptions to recovering true spiritual health:

1. *Look to Christ* both to define your condition and to provide the cure—"I counsel you to buy from me gold refined by fire, so that you may be rich, and white garments so that you may clothe yourself and the shame of your nakedness may not be seen, and salve to anoint your eyes, so that you may see" (v 18).

2. *"Be zealous" (v 19).* The word *zealous* literally means "boiling," and it is in the present tense. Jesus commands the Laodiceans—and us—to make it a continual practice to keep the fire of their spiritual devotion burning.

3. *"Repent" (v 19).* The word *repent* calls us to recognize the truth about our condition and then to do something about it! Jesus is telling the Laodiceans to stop pretending they are spiritually mature and to wake up to the reality that they are in a desperate condition.

4. *Open the door*—"Behold, I stand at the door and knock. If anyone hears my voice and opens the door, I will come in to him and eat with him, and he with me" (v 20). Though usually applied to unbelievers and seekers, these words are really addressed to believers who have lost the fiery passion of their faith.

The cure for spiritual mediocrity is not redoubling our efforts, increasing our devotional life, or attending more conferences. The only remedy for a lukewarm heart is to open the door and let Jesus come in (see vv 20–21)!

Laodicea at a Glance

Historical Context	Laodicea was one of the wealthiest cities in the Roman Empire.
Titles of Christ	"The words of the Amen, the faithful and true witness, the beginning of God's creation" (Rev 3:14).
Commendations	None

Rebukes	"I know your works: you are neither cold nor hot. Would that you were either cold or hot!...You are lukewarm....you say, I am rich, I have prospered, and I need nothing, not realizing that you are wretched, pitiable, poor, blind, and naked" (Rev 3:15–17).
Commands	"Buy from me gold refined by fire...and white garments...and salve....be zealous and repent." (Rev 3:18–19)
Warnings	"I will spit you out of my mouth....I reprove and discipline" (Rev 3:16, 19).
Promises	"If anyone hears my voice and opens the door, I will come in to him and eat with him, and he with me. The one who conquers, I will grant him to sit with me on my throne...." (Rev 3:20–21).
Major Theme	Jesus is looking for followers full of zeal and fiery passion. Lukewarmness makes him nauseated.
Message for Us	Beware "Goldilocks" Christians—those who want a faith that is neither too hot nor too cold, but tepid and lukewarm.

Insights for Today's Church

As noted earlier, these short pastoral letters to the seven churches of Asia have direct application to our congregations of the twenty-first century. While each letter contains a specific message for a specific situation, the larger message is found in viewing them together. So what can we learn from these letters that will help us in our churches today?

First, remember the Lord stands "in the midst of" the lampstands, the churches (1:12–13). Even though some of these churches are sinful, heretical, or dysfunctional, the risen Christ still identifies with the churches that bear his name. Don't be too quick to write off a congregation that is struggling. Don't give up on a church until Christ does.

Second, each individual church can reveal only a part of who Christ is, so it takes many kinds of congregations to manifest the full glory of his work in this world. Thus we learn the unique value of each individual congregation and at the same time the indispensable value of the larger community of churches (see 1 Cor 12:11–27).

Third, the Lord intends to place each of us in a *community* of faith. In the words of John Wesley, the Lord does not expect us to be "holy solitaries." We are members of the family of God, yet our personal responsibility remains. One can be lost in a good congregation just as one can be saved in a bad one.

Fourth, the church is a lampstand. Its purpose is to radiate the light of Christ to the nations. The church is called to expose what hides in the darkness. It must be the conscience of the world.

Fifth, the destiny of the cosmos unfolds in the life of the church—not in Washington, at Harvard, on Wall Street, in Hollywood, or at the Pentagon. Jesus is preparing his Bride for her wedding day. When the Bride is ready, the End will come (see 19:7).

Sixth, church life today appears quite different from church life in John's day. It is remarkable how Revelation is silent concerning many of the priorities of contemporary churches. Things such as organizational structure, leadership hierarchy, programs, buildings, and styles of worship are not even mentioned. Rather, these letters emphasize foundational realities such as faithfulness in persecution, correctness in doctrine, and purity in moral conduct.

Finally, when the church falls short of what the Lord expects it to be, we need to wake up. We see this prescription again and again in these letters: Remember, repent, and do the works you did at first. Hold fast. Be zealous. Open the door. If we fail to respond in this manner, the church's candlestick just might be removed (see 2:5)!

But for those who walk in obedient faith and remain steadfast in adversity, the promised rewards are great:

- We will eat of "the tree of life" (2:7), will wear crowns, and will not be hurt by the second death (see 2:10–11).
- We will be given "authority over the nations" (2:26), and the non-believing world will bow before us and will understand that God loves us (see 3:9).
- We will be clothed in white garments, our names will not be blotted from the Book of Life, and Jesus will confess our names before the Father (see 3:4–5).

For Reflection and Discussion

1. Which of the seven churches does your church most resemble?
2. What heresies are troubling the church today?
3. What is God asking you to do? What false teachings or ungodly lifestyles should you confront and condemn?
4. What conclusion should we draw from the fact that most (all?) of the seven churches addressed in this book no longer exist?
5. How do you keep yourself from becoming spiritually dead or lukewarm?

3.
A Glimpse through the Door
(Rev 4:1–5:14)

When Adam and Eve were expelled from their home in the Garden of Eden, the way back was blocked by an angel with a flaming sword (see Gen 3:24). Ever since then, their children have lived somewhere "east of Eden" (Gen 4:16) wandering aimlessly in the land of Nod ("wandering" in Hebrew), groping for the door that would lead them back to life as it was meant to be. The Tower of Babel was the first human attempt to find the door that would once again permit access to man's true home. Building a ziggurat with a stairway they hoped would reach "the gate of heaven" (Gen 11:1–11), the builders soon learned their efforts were futile. The dramatic failure of this enterprise became an eternal object lesson: we can never find the way to heaven in our own strength and piety.

Later in Genesis, we read the story of Jacob's ladder, or stairway (see Gen 28:10–22). This was God's solution to a problem man could not fix. Yes, there is indeed an opening, a door, between this world and the next, but only God can show us how to find it. And only God has the key to open and close the door. The gospel announces that Jesus himself is not only *the ladder* (see John 1:51) but also *the door* that connects us to the very presence of God (see John 10:7–10). There is only one door, only one way to connect with the other world: Jesus Christ. He is the way. No one comes to the Father except through him (see John 14:6). The door is narrow (see Luke 13:22–30), but it leads to glorious life, vast and abundant. Finding the door is the most important goal in life!

Ezekiel's vision (Ezek 1:1), Jesus' baptism (Matt 3:16), Stephen's martyrdom (Acts 7:56), and the Gentiles' being welcomed into God's family

(Acts 10:11) are pivotal moments in Scripture when "the heavens were opened" and humans were enabled to get a glimpse through the door that connects this world to the Kingdom of Heaven. The book of Revelation has much to say about doors and the keys that open them. It describes several occasions when the heavens are opened and the other world interacts with this world (see 1:18; 3:7–8, 20; 11:19; 19:11). In Revelation 4:1, John sees "a door standing open in heaven!" As he looks through the door, he begins to gain an understanding of God's purposes for the church and for the world.

A Heavenly Invitation

Hearing a voice from heaven like a trumpet, John receives an amazing invitation: "Come up here, and I will show you what must take place after this" (4:1). John sees heaven not as a temple but as the throne room of the Lord God Almighty (see 4:8). Though someone was sitting on the throne, John seems at first unable to describe him. Rather, he fixates on the bright light reflected from precious stones (jasper, carnelian, and emerald) surrounding the throne. The light appears as a rainbow (see 4:3), reminding us of God's covenant with Noah. Though disaster is coming on the earth, God has not forgotten his promise to preserve his faithful people.

John then notices 24 elders seated on 24 thrones surrounding the central throne of God (see 4:4). The number 24 probably signifies the 12 tribes of the Old Covenant and the 12 apostles of the New (see 21:12–14). They wear white robes, which connote their redemption through the blood of the Lamb (see 7:14). They are also wearing crowns and are seated on thrones, indicating that they share the royal sovereign reign with the one seated on the central throne. John also sees four living creatures around the throne: a lion, an ox, a man, and an eagle in flight (see 4:7). Each of them has six wings, reminiscent of the creatures Isaiah saw surrounding God in the temple (see Isa 6:1–2). The elders and creatures are singing praises to God, falling down in worship, and casting their crowns before his throne to signify their complete surrender to him (see 4:8–10).

So far, there is nothing distinctively "Christian" about what John is seeing in heaven. In chapter 4, heavenly beings are worshiping God for all that he has done in creation: "for you created all things, and by your will they existed and were created" (4:11). Such a vision of heaven could have conceivably been written by any other pious Jew. However, when we turn to chapter 5, the picture of heaven becomes Christ-centered and thoroughly "Christian." Here we see the Lamb that was slain and realize that worship is no longer is focused upon all God has done in creation but rather upon all God has done in redemption. "For you were slain, and by your blood you ransomed people for God from every tribe and language and people and nation" (5:9–10).

Who Can Open the Scroll?

John focuses his attention on a great scroll (see 5:1–5). We soon learn that this scroll contains a detailed account of what God is about to do. It describes the destiny of the world. Until the scroll is opened, the future remains a mystery and God's purposes cannot become manifest. But who can open the seals of the scroll? Who is worthy for such a task? John weeps at the thought that there is no one in the universe who is able to take the scroll from the hand of the one seated on the throne and open it so that God's purposes might be finally fulfilled. Then one of the elders says, "Weep no more; behold, the Lion of the tribe of Judah, the Root of David, has conquered, so that he can open the scroll and its seven seals" (5:5).

Looking for a lion to appear, John is shocked to see a lamb instead! And this lamb appears "as though it had been slain" (5:6). Those familiar with the New Testament will recognize immediately that John is seeing none other than the Second Person of the Trinity, the Son of God, Jesus Christ. But is he a lion or a lamb? John's vision merges the two realities so

that the being John sees is a lion-like lamb—or is it a lamb-like lion? When this glorious being appears, the four creatures and 24 elders fall down to worship him, singing this song:

> *Worthy are you to take the scroll and to open its seals,*
> *for you were slain, and by your blood you ransomed people for God*
> *from every tribe and language and people and nation,*
> *and you have made them a kingdom and priests to our God,*
> *and they shall reign on the earth. (5:9–10)*

Note it well: when John peers through the door of heaven to see what is happening on the other side, he sees worship! Every act of corporate worship on earth is preparation for the glorious future when the entire universe joins in the adoration and praise of him who sits on the throne. Worship in the throne room of heaven is the prototype for all genuine worship everywhere. Notice the three essential elements of worship:

1. *Seeing God truly.* All worship is centered on the one seated on the throne and preeminently on the Lamb who bears the wounds of his sacrificial death.

2. *Praising God passionately.* No one is bored in this worship. No one is falling asleep. In the heavenly worship service, there is weeping, bowing, and lots of singing. Worship is meant to be a spine-tingling, breath-taking, heart-pounding, white-knuckle experience.

3. *Offering ourselves completely.* The worshipers in heaven cast their crowns before the throne, because true worship always involves surrendering everything to the Lamb.

If you find worship to be a boring experience, you are going to be miserable in heaven! Every time we gather for worship on Sunday morning, we are having a dress rehearsal for eternity.

Notice that the last word of worship in the throne room of heaven is "Amen" (5:14). Though written in Greek, John is using a transliteration of a Hebrew term frequently used in Jewish worship. "Amen" means something is "firm, dependable, durable, and lasting." It denotes certainty and truth. Thus, to say "Amen" after a prayer, a hymn, or a service of worship means you agree with what has just been said and affirm it. Saying "Amen" makes it binding for you.

Jesus used this word often; in fact, there are 63 occurrences of it in the four gospels. He often used this word to emphasize the truth of what he said: "Amen, Amen, I say to you" (translated "Verily, verily" [KJV], or "Truly, truly" [ESV]). It was Jesus' way of saying, "So be it!" Likewise, when we say "Amen" in worship, it is our way of underscoring the fact that our declarations of praise for who God is and what he has done are the truest things we will ever say!

In recent years, we have seen a lot of conflict in American churches over worship. These "worship wars" can get quite emotional and even ugly. They tend to focus on things such as instruments and styles of music used in church. If you are tempted to enter into these kinds of battles, let me encourage you to look again at Revelation 4–5. Here you will find worship in its absolute purity and beauty. Do all possible to make the worship in your church resemble the worship in the throne room of heaven!

For Reflection and Discussion

1. Describe a typical worship service in your congregation. How is it similar to the worship of heaven? How is it different?

2. Revelation 4–5 speaks of worshiping God for his work in creation and worshiping the Lamb for his work in redemption. Does your church affirm both realities in its Sunday worship services?

3. Have you been involved in the "worship wars" of recent years? How has this study confirmed your ideas about worship or changed them?

4. How does John's description of God's throne room comfort and encourage you?

5. How does your personal worship experience compare to that of the creatures in heaven? Are you bored during worship or a full, willing participant?

6. How does your image of Jesus—Lion or Lamb—affect your worship?

4.

Who Can Stand?

(Rev 6:1–17)

When I was growing up, the boys in my neighborhood sometimes played a game called "Last Man Standing." There really weren't any rules. The object of the game was simple: tackle everyone else before they tackled you so you could be the last man standing! In playing the game, I often imagined that I was General George Armstrong Custer at the Battle of Little Bighorn. Standing tall, proud, and heroic, he epitomized the ideal of being the last man to fall. But of course, he, too, finally hit the ground.

The sixth chapter of Revelation describes a series of events that make the Battle of Little Bighorn seem trivial in comparison. As six of the seven seals are opened, one by one, a series of judgments falls upon the earth. The four horsemen of the Apocalypse arrive, and the final judgment begins. As the fury of God's wrath is unleashed upon this sinful planet, kings and generals, the rich and powerful, and everyone both slave and free look desperately for shelter in rocks and caves, crying out in anguish as they ask one haunting question: "Who can stand?" (6:15–17). In this chapter, John gives us a picture of "the wrath of the Lamb" (6:16). No one can stand before his righteous fury. When history reaches its final consummation and the dust settles from Armageddon's conclusive battle, the Lamb of God will indeed be the Last Man Standing!

In the ancient world, an important document was often sealed so that its authority would be immediately obvious and its contents protected from those who had no right to know what it said. For a scroll, the seal was typically hot wax or clay, a kind of glue that kept the document rolled up and closed. It wasn't the strength of the adhesive that provided the security,

as most seals were easily broken. Rather, it was the imprint in the wax that would cause any would-be intruder to pause. When the wax was first applied, it was moist, giving the one who wrote the document the chance to affix his personal symbol, often using a signet ring to press his mark into the clay. Anyone opening the scroll without permission would know that he would one day have to give an account to the owner of the scroll, the one whose insignia he had violated. To open a sealed scroll written by a great king would be a treasonable offense unless the one opening the scroll had been given authority to do so.

In John's vision, the one seated on the throne holds a scroll in his right hand, sealed with seven seals (see 5:1). This scroll, written on front and back, explains the future destiny of the world. Only one person in the entire universe is worthy to open the seals: the Lamb that had been slain (see 5:5–7). As each seal is opened, one by one, an escalation of divine wrath and judgment is released upon the earth.

The First Four Seals: Four Horsemen (Rev 6:1–8)

The first four seals release four horses, whose riders are often called the Four Horsemen of the Apocalypse. Don't spend too much time trying to figure out the precise identity of these horsemen or the time period they may represent. That doesn't seem to be the point of the vision. The Christians to whom John was writing likely would have understood these horsemen to be a general summary of human history, which has typically been characterized by conquest, wars, violence, famines, disease, death, and natural disasters. This is precisely what these four horsemen bring. The vision is to be experienced and felt more than it is to be analyzed.

When the first seal is opened, a white horsemen is released (see 6:1–2). Its rider has a bow and is wearing a crown. But who is this rider, and what does the white horse represent? Some think this is a picture of Jesus Christ, because later in the book we see him riding a white horse when he returns in power and glory (see 19:11ff). However, it seems more likely that this first horseman is Satan himself. Because he is able to disguise himself as an angel of light (see 2 Cor 11:14), Satan comes camouflaged so that many will mistake him for Christ. He comes "conquering, and to conquer." Satan's goal is world conquest and a kingdom where he reigns supreme.

The second horse is fiery red (see 6:3–4). Red here seems to symbolize blood. This horseman is carrying a great sword and spreads warfare and violence over the earth. He is given permission "to take peace from the earth, so that people should slay one another."

The third horseman is riding a black horse (see 6:5–6), which brings famine to the earth. He is carrying a pair of scales so that the earth's food provisions can be carefully rationed. It takes a day's wage to purchase a quart of wheat, which is what it takes to keep one person alive. Families will have to eat the less nourishing barley, because it is cheaper. A day's wage is enough to buy three quarts, which would provide subsistence living for a small family. Notice that this horseman does not allow anyone to "harm the oil and wine," apparently because these are considered luxury items. The rich can enjoy oil and wine while the poor expend all their energies just to survive. This sounds like much of human history, doesn't it? In Africa today, people are dying of malnutrition, while in America, we are dying of obesity.

The fourth horse is a pale horse (see 6:7–8). Its ashen color reminds us of disease and death, which is what he brings to the world. The rider is identified as "death" and following close behind is another figure named "Hades" (Hell). These evil characters are permitted to kill one fourth of the world's population by the sword, famine, plague, and wild beasts.

Human history illustrates in small measure what these four horsemen will one day bring to the entire earth. No one will escape the impact of these four horsemen.

The Fifth Seal: the Altar (Rev 6:9–11)

When the fifth seal is opened, John sees a massive altar, and under it are "the souls of those who had been slain for the word of God and for the witness they had borne" (v 9). This seal has unleashed a tidal wave of persecution against the people of God. Thousands upon thousands are being killed for their faith. Though such persecution has typified the past two thousand years, never has it been more true than today. But in the days to come, things will get much worse. No wonder the martyrs cry out, "O Sovereign Lord, holy and true, how long…?" (v 10). Lord, will our suffering never end? When will you bring judgment on the wicked and avenge our blood? This is the cry of the suffering church that has been brutalized, victimized, and terrorized by thugs and murderers for centuries. It is not a cry for revenge, but rather a cry that God will vindicate his name in the earth. God's response to the martyrs' question reassures them of his coming help and deliverance. But the necessity of waiting "a little longer" (v 11) is at the same time a call to endure.

The Sixth Seal: Calamity and Catastrophe (Rev 6:12–17)

The opening of the sixth seal lets loose a series of worldwide calamities and catastrophes, some of them of cosmic proportions: there is a great earthquake, the sun turns black, the moon turns to blood, the stars fall from the heavens, the sky is rolled back as a scroll, and the mountains and the islands are removed. This sixth seal is so terrible that everyone on earth—kings and generals, the rich and the powerful, and slaves and freemen—is running in panic and hiding in caves, pleading for someone to protect them from "the face of him who is seated on the throne, and from the wrath of the Lamb" (6:16). How ironic! What terrifies these noble souls is *not* war, famine, disease, earthquakes, or even death. What terrifies them is God's face, turned in anger against them, and the wrath of the Lamb!

Sanctified Anger

It requires a sanctified imagination to picture how an angry lamb can terrify kings and generals! Yet this image illustrates several important truths about the place for righteous anger in our world today. Many evangelicals seem to have been taught that anger is always bad and should be avoided at all costs. They seem to equate anger with hatred, vindictiveness, spite, rage, loss of temper, and the like. But on at least three occasions, Jesus, during his life on earth, got angry. His cheeks flushed, the veins on his neck stood out, he shouted, and his words had an edge on them. While many of us tend to associate such demonstrative emotions with sin, we can be sure this was not the case with the spotless Lamb of God! Notice both the things that provoked anger in Jesus and how he expressed it. Jesus got angry when:

- People hardened their hearts and willfully made a conscious choice to reject the truth (see Mark 3:5).
- His disciples hindered children from coming into his presence (see Mark 10:14).
- Religious people used religion to camouflage their own selfish ambition (see John 2:13–17).

The wrath of the Lamb may not be a popular concept, but it is a fact. Either you will face an angry Lamb now and allow his blood to wash you clean from the sins that arouse his wrath, or you will deal with an angry Lamb at the final judgment, when it will be too late to do anything about it! The choice is yours.

But there's more. The cleansing blood of Jesus and the sanctifying Spirit of Pentecost mean that *we* are now able to express anger even as Jesus did. In fact, God *expects* us to be angry at the same things and in the same way as Jesus. Righteous indignation is part of the *image of God* that needs expression in and through the lives of the redeemed. This is why we are encouraged to "be angry and do not sin" (Eph 4:26). No, we are not to avenge ourselves when we are wronged. We must leave that matter with God (see Rom 12:19–21). But we are to allow the righteous indignation, the sanctified anger, aroused by the presence of sin in our world to motivate us to address and confront instances of injustice and oppression all around us.

For Reflection and Discussion

1. Describe your own thoughts and feelings about the wrath of God. How has this study challenged your understanding of God and the Lamb of God?

2. Do you think of martyrdom as part of the normal Christian life? Why or why not?

3. What makes Jesus angry? How does he express it? What makes you angry? How do you express it?

4. Where are Christians full of sanctified anger needed in the world today?

5.
Safe and Secure
(Rev 7:1–17)

Chapter 7 provides a sort of intermission, a pregnant pause between the opening of the sixth seal (see 6:12) and the seventh (see 8:1ff). This interval of time provides the opportunity to answer the question: what is going to happen to followers of the Lamb during these days of destruction and wrath coming on the world? John has a vision where he sees things on earth (see 7:1–8) and then things in heaven (see 7:9–17). While no one on the earth is able to stand before the wrath of the Lamb (see 6:16–17), surprisingly, John's vision reveals that some are indeed able to stand! But who they are and why they are still standing may surprise you.

- "After this I saw four angels *standing* at the four corners of the earth…" (7:1)
- "After this I looked, and behold a great multitude…*standing* before the throne and before the Lamb…" (7:9)
- "And all the angels were *standing* around the throne and around the elders and the four living creatures, and they fell on their faces before the throne and worshiped God." (7:11)

The only ones able to stand when judgment comes on the earth are those who worship the one seated on the throne and the Lamb. But even they don't stand for long because of their freely chosen decision to offer praise and worship to their Redeemer. Rather than awaiting the day of judgment, when God's enemies will fall in terror, the redeemed make a choice to fall on their faces before the Lamb in adoration and praise. Yes, the day is coming soon when "every knee [will] bow, in heaven and on earth and under the earth, and every tongue confess that Jesus Christ is

Lord, to the glory of God the Father" (Phil 2:10–11). The ultimate question of life thus becomes: will I fall before him of my own free will, or will I fall before him in terror, suddenly realizing I waited too long?

John's First Vision (Rev 7:1–8)

In the first vision, John sees four angels standing at the four corners of the earth. They are temporarily "holding back" the destructive events about to be released on the world. But something of great importance needs to happen before the terrors are unleashed: the servants of God must first be sealed. In other words, as the scroll is *unsealed*, the saints are *sealed!* As judgments fall on the earth, God is clearly marking those who belong to him. Once the saints are marked by the protective seal of God, the seventh seal can be opened (see 8:1) and the final judgment can begin.

An angel appears, carrying "the seal of the living God" (v 2). Apparently, this is the same seal that had been used to seal the scroll that had just been opened, releasing the divine judgments on the earth. Now God wants to take this same seal (perhaps an insignia or signet ring) and mark the foreheads of the 144,000 true believers still alive on the earth. The number 144,000 is almost certainly symbolic, being related to the 12 tribes of Israel (see vv 4–8). It is also the product of three perfect numbers (12 x 12 x 1,000). The emphasis seems to be on the *completeness* of the number of those being saved rather than the exact mathematical calculation. When we come to the second part of John's vision, we discover that the 144,000 seem to morph into a "great multitude that no one could number" (v 9).

John's Second Vision (Rev 7:9–17)

The second part of John's vision occurs in heaven, where John sees a vast congregation worshiping the one seated on the throne. It seems probable that John wants us to understand that these persons received the seal of God on their foreheads while they still lived on the earth. The congregation is composed of an innumerable throng of worshipers from every nation, tribe, and language "standing before the throne and before the Lamb" (v 9). John notices that they are all wearing white robes. It is important to point out that, in heaven, God's people will not return to some Eden-like garden where they will be naked, as some philosophers of nudism like to pretend. Innocence, once lost, cannot be restored. But sins can be gloriously forgiven! Our guilt and shame can be covered. In heaven, their robes are white because they have been washed—they were dirty once—in the blood of the Lamb (see v 14). It takes a sanctified imagination to understand how red blood can make dirty garments sparkling white! Dressed in white and carrying palm branches, the great congregation of the redeemed lift their voices in united praise: "Salvation belongs to our God who sits on the throne, and to the Lamb" (v 10).

When John asks from where this great multitude has come, he is told that "these are the ones coming out of the great tribulation" (v 14). Though many today want to believe that Christians will be raptured away to eternal bliss *before* the Great Tribulation comes upon the earth, it is important to recognize that this passage clearly states that God's people will be saved *through* tribulation, not *from* it! (See also John 16:33; Acts 14:22.)

Heaven is a place of "shelter" (v 15) where the redeemed can take refuge in the very presence of God from the judgments and punishments that ravage the earth. The Lamb will "shepherd" his sheep (v 17), and all their needs will be graciously met. God himself will "wipe away every tear from their eyes" (v 17).

Which Seal Marks You?

John tells us that as divine judgment falls on the earth, God marks his children with a seal so their identity is clear and they are protected from the wrath to come (see 7:2–3; 9:4; 14:1; 22:4). But Satan also has a diabolical plan to designate his followers. Just as God's servants are marked on

their foreheads, Satan puts a counterfeit "mark of the Beast" on those who belong to him.

> *And [the false prophet] causes all, both small and great, both rich and poor, both free and slave, to be marked on the right hand or the forehead, so that no one can buy or sell unless he has the mark, that is, the name of the beast or the number of its name. This calls for wisdom: let the one who has understanding calculate the number of the beast, for it is the number of a man, and his number is 666. (13:16–18)*

Our eternal destiny hinges upon one question: to whom do we belong? Whose mark (or seal) do we bear? Those sealed with the mark of the Beast will be thrown into the lake of fire (see 20:14), while those marked with the seal of God will be taken to heaven (see 14:1; 22:4).

God's seal does for a human soul what a wax seal does for an official document: it authenticates it and guarantees that the contents belong to the King. Anyone who dares to tamper with the King's property will give an account for such effrontery. Notice that such a seal does not protect a royal document from danger, harm, or pain. But it does guarantee its final preservation. Christians are promised deliverance from wrath and judgment, not from tribulation and pain.

The book of Revelation is perhaps the greatest work of pastoral theology ever written. Pastor John was writing to help his people survive and thrive in an evil world. The sealing of the saints may not spare us from adversity, but it will guarantee our final and ultimate victory through the blood of the Lamb!

How to Be Sealed by God

In light of the judgment coming on the world, few questions are more important than these: How can I be sealed by God? How can I be safe and secure from the wrath to come? How can I have the blessed assurance that

I am his and he is mine? Such questions require a twofold answer.

First, you must have a robe, and it must be washed white in the blood of the Lamb (see 7:14). Until we have received by faith the benefits that flow from the cross of Jesus Christ, notably forgiveness for our sinful actions, we simply cannot have assurance that our identity in Christ is secure. It is only when our guilt is removed that we can be sealed with the mark that assures us of our standing before God. Isaiah put it powerfully when he said, "Come now, let us reason together, says the LORD: though your sins are like scarlet, they shall be as white as snow; though they are red like crimson, they shall become like wool" (Isa 1:18).

Nikolaus von Zinzendorf wrote a remarkable hymn in 1739 that speaks of our white robes of righteousness made possible by the death of Christ. John Wesley translated the hymn from German into English a year later. Following are three verses of this great hymn:

Jesus, Thy blood and righteousness
My beauty are, my glorious dress;
'Midst flaming worlds, in these arrayed,
With joy shall I lift up my head.

Lord, I believe were sinners more
Than sands upon the ocean shore,
Thou hast for all a ransom paid,
For all a full atonement made.

This spotless robe the same appears,
When ruined nature sinks in years;
No age can change its glorious hue,
The robe of Christ is ever new.

Second, you must receive the Holy Spirit. Paul seems to equate the sealing of God with the infilling of the Holy Spirit:

In him you also, when you heard the word of truth, the gospel of your salvation, and believed in him, were sealed with the promised Holy Spirit, who is the guarantee of our inheritance until we acquire possession of it, to the praise of his glory. (Eph 1:13–14)

When we are filled with the Holy Spirit, we receive the mark of his ownership: we are sealed. Furthermore, our future is safe and secure as we rest in the faith that he will guard and protect all those he has purchased with his blood. The Spirit's infilling then makes possible a transformation of our hearts and minds so that the image of God is restored in the lives of the redeemed (see Rom 12:1–2; Col 3:10).

For Reflection and Discussion

1. How do you understand the "sealing" work of the Holy Spirit? Has this study changed your thinking or confirmed it?

2. How do you respond to this statement: Christians are saved *through* tribulation, not *from* it? How does it fit your experience?

3. In Revelation, the saints were sealed by a mark on their foreheads, obvious to all. Is your identity, your seal, obvious to others? Why or why not?

4. Do you have full assurance of your standing before God? Do you feel safe and secure?

6.
Holy Smoke
(Rev 8:1–9:21; 11:15–19)

As the Lamb opens the six seals (see 6:1–17), the destiny of the world unfolds, one terrifying event at a time: war, famine, disease, death, persecution, etc. As we have examined these catastrophes, it has not always been clear whether John was describing past events, current events, or events still to come. However, with the opening of the seventh seal (see 8:1), we clearly are dealing with realities yet in the future, both for John and for us. You may think life on planet Earth has been difficult as it is portrayed by the first six seals, but wait till you see what happens when the seventh seal is opened and the seven trumpets start to blow!

A Pregnant Pause

When the Lamb opens the seventh and final seal, there is "silence in heaven for about half an hour" (8:1). What a dramatic moment! What a pregnant pause! Until this point, Revelation has been a very noisy book: huge choirs, thunder, earthquakes, and galloping horses. But now, a deafening silence! In a crowded room, even two or three minutes of silence can seem like an eternity. Imagine the impact of thirty minutes of silence while millions of citizens of heaven hold their breath, waiting to see what God will do next. In the silence, two things are happening:

1. God is listening to the prayers of his people arising from the earth like smoke—holy smoke (see 8:3–5).

2. Seven angels are issued seven trumpets (see 8:2).

God listens closely to the prayers of his people still suffering on the earth (see 8:3–5). The catastrophic results of the first six seals affect

Christians as well as unbelievers. They, too, experience the war, violence, famine, and persecution that has been let loose on the world. The silence in heaven seems to enhance God's "ability" to listen to his people praying on the earth. And "the smoke of the incense, with the prayers of the saints, rose before God" (8:4). What happens next is dramatic. An angel takes the censer that has been used to offer the prayers to God and fills it "with fire from the altar" (8:5). These fiery coals are thrown down onto the earth, breaking the silence with "peals of thunder, rumblings, flashes of lightning, and an earthquake" (8:5). As the prayers, like smoke, rise silently upward, the fire of judgment comes down with a loud boom!

Something else is happening in heaven during these thirty minutes of silence. Seven angels are given seven trumpets (see 8:2). Whether a curved ram's horn (*shophar*) or a long, straight metallic instrument, trumpets in the Bible are used to:

- Call the people together.
- Warn of danger.
- Prepare for battle.
- Celebrate victories, holidays, and feasts.
- Announce the arrival of royalty.

The seven angels prepare to blow their seven trumpets one after another. Six of the trumpets are blown in rapid succession, each announcing a plague upon the earth (see 8:6–9:21). These plagues are far worse than the plagues of Egypt (see Ex 7–12).

The *first trumpet* (see 8:7) causes hail and fire mixed with blood to fall on the earth. One-third of the earth is burned up. The *second trumpet* (see 8:8–9) affects the salt waters of the earth. A mountain of fire thrown into the sea brings cataclysmic destruction. With the sounding of the *third trumpet* (see 8:10–11), a blazing star named Wormwood falls on the fresh waters of the earth. Many die due to the toxic condition of the water. The *fourth trumpet* (see 8:12) affects the heavens as one-third of the sun, moon, and stars are struck and one-third of all light is darkened.

Before the final three trumpets are blown, a brief interlude occurs. An eagle appears in the sky, crying out in a loud voice, "Woe, woe, woe to those who dwell on the earth, at the blasts of the other trumpets that the three angels are about to blow!" (8:13). The blowing of the final three trumpets announces the arrival of three woes, ushering in a time of unfathomable suffering on the earth.

The fifth angel blows his trumpet, which announces the first woe (see 9:1–12). John's vision of "a star fallen from heaven to earth" (9:1) is probably a description of Satan (Lucifer) and his expulsion from heaven (see Isa 14:12; Luke 10:18; Rev 12:7–12). Upon being given the key to the shaft to the bottomless pit, this fallen angel releases swarms of locusts upon the earth. Though biblical history describes other occasions when locusts are used for divine judgment (see Ex 10:1–20; Joel 1:4; 2:5), this is undoubtedly the worst! The locusts are specifically commanded *not* to harm the vegetation "but only those people who do not have the seal of God on their foreheads" (9:4). The real explanation for the five-month reign of terror brought on the earth by this demonic infestation of locusts is that their king is none other than Apollyon (Greek), or Abaddon (Hebrew). In both languages, the word means "the Destroyer." Yet in the midst of this devastating plague, note that those sealed by God are protected from direct harm by these locusts. God's saints suffer, but their suffering is limited in comparison to the rest of the world.

As the sixth angel blows his trumpet, which is the second woe (see 9:13–21), an army of 200 million mounted troops come forth and kill a third of the earth's population. The riders wear "breastplates the color of fire and of sapphire and of sulfur" (9:17), but their horses provoke the greatest fear. With heads like lions and tails like biting serpents, each horse breathes out of its mouth fire, smoke, and sulfur.

Tragically, those who survive the destruction caused by the first six trumpets continue in their sinful behaviors and refuse to repent (see

9:20–21). Even at this late hour, God longs to show mercy and grace and to forgive sin so that judgment can be averted. The purpose of these plagues and catastrophes is not merely punitive. They come with the hope that they can waken sinners from their slumber and bring rebels to repentance. "The Lord is not slow to fulfill his promise as some count slowness, but is patient toward you, not wishing that any should perish, but that all should reach repentance" (2 Pet 3:9).

As the six trumpets blow, it feels like all hell is breaking loose. It is! But when we skip ahead to chapter 11 to discover what happens when the seventh trumpet is blown, we discover a radically different reality as the culmination of human history is gloriously proclaimed:

> *Then the seventh angel blew his trumpet, and there were loud voices in heaven, saying, "The kingdom of the world has become the kingdom of our Lord and of his Christ, and he shall reign forever and ever." (11:15)*

The seventh trumpet announces that God has taken authority and has begun to reign. The time has come for God's servants to be rewarded and for the destroyers to be destroyed (see 11:17–18). The interval between the final two trumpets (see 10:1–11:14) is a description of yet another opportunity God extends to sinners to repent and be saved from the wrath to come. We'll examine this opportunity in the next chapter.

The Power of Prayer

Perhaps the most important lesson we can draw from Revelation 8, 9, and 11 has to do neither with the sequence of end-time events nor their intensity, as some might argue. Rather, this passage of Scripture should be seen as a call to prayer. These chapters are as much about the power of prayer as they are about the end of the world. The angels in heaven blew their trumpets only because God's people on earth said their prayers! As prayer rose silently to heaven like incense smoke, God signaled the angels to blow their trumpets. Only as the prayers of God's people go up does the fire of God's judgment come down. Pastor John wants to encourage his little flock, living in an evil empire, to use their ultimate weapon. Indeed, prayer has always been the believer's nuclear option.

As we close this chapter, let's draw out the lessons on prayer that Pastor John would give us as we face the challenges of the evil day in which we live.

First, *never underestimate the power of prayer*. Rising smoke is silent; it makes no sound. But in heaven, God is listening and is preparing to cast fire on the earth. In the late 1970s, a delegation from the World Council of Churches visited Russia to report on the state of the church under the Communist regime. The delegates were not impressed. Their report coldly stated, "It's just a bunch of old ladies praying." Little did they realize the power that was being released as those humble *babushkas* went quietly about their daily prayers! Twenty years later, the Soviet Union crumbled in ruins, and the world wondered why. Thugs and tyrants everywhere should tremble when "old ladies" pray! The real revolutionaries in this world are not found in Washington, Wall Street, Harvard, or Hollywood. To discover those who have the power to change the world, go to a prayer meeting!

Second, *no prayer is wasted*. The angel's censer had to be filled with coals before it was cast down upon the earth (see 8:3–5). In other words, God's judgments are released upon the earth only when the "prayer bucket" is full of the petitions and intercessions of his saints. Don't stop praying! Your prayer may be the one that fills the bucket and signals God to act.

Third, *prayer is pleasing to God*. The smoke of the prayers of the saints that ascends to the throne room of heaven is mixed with incense (see 8:3–4), making a pleasing aroma to God. God loves it when we pray!

Little Boy kneels at the foot of the bed,

Droops on the little hands little gold head.

Hush! Hush! whisper who dares!

Christopher Robin is saying his prayers.[10]

Fourth, *prayer changes history.* Prayer is so much more than pious contemplation and a search for inner peace. Prayer has the capacity to move mountains and to change the course of history. Never underestimate the power of prayer!

Finally, *prayer moves God to bring people to repentance.* While we like to imagine that our intercessions for the lost actually make life better for them, we need to remember that sometimes God responds to our petitions for others by letting all hell break loose in their lives. There is nothing like suffering to bring a person to repentance. In many cases, pain and hardship seem to be God's final and ultimate methods for creating the opportunity for someone to repent and believe. No one has said this better than C. S. Lewis in his classic book *The Problem of Pain*[11]: "God whispers to us in our pleasures, speaks in our conscience, but shouts in our pain: it is His megaphone to rouse a deaf world." So go ahead and pray for your unsaved family and friends, but be prepared for the crisis your prayers may produce!

For Reflection and Discussion

1. How has this chapter affected your attitude toward prayer?
2. How will your prayer life be different because of the lessons in this chapter?
3. What should be a Christian's attitude toward suffering in light of its redemptive possibilities for non-believers?
4. What brought you to a place of repentance?

---

10 A. A. Milne, *Vespers* (Hollywood: Chappell Music, 1924), n.p.

11 C. S. Lewis, *The Problem of Pain* (Glasgow: Collins, 1940), 74.

7.

Can I Get a Witness?
(Rev 10:1–11:14)

On the Niagara River just above the falls is a place known as "The Point of No Return." Here the current is so strong and swift that even the most powerful motorboat cannot overcome the pull of the water. Beyond this point, going over the falls is inevitable; the fate of the boat and its passengers is sealed.

In the first nine chapters of Revelation, we read about various judgments and plagues coming upon the earth. Throughout this period, men and women still have the opportunity to turn from their sin and get right with God. It's not too late to "flee from the wrath to come" (Matt 3:7). But when the seventh trumpet is blown (see 11:15ff), the world has reached the point of no return. From this point forward, the fate of those who are not right with God seems to be forever sealed. They will be swept up in the current of destruction that is coming on the earth. There will be no escape. Revelation 10:1–11:14 represents God's final invitation to turn from sin and trust in the Lamb. You can hear the thunderous roar of final judgment in the distance. Literally, it's now or never. At the conclusion of these two chapters, the seventh trumpet is blown and human destinies are fixed forever. (To be strictly accurate, God does offer one brief and final invitation to salvation in Revelation 14:6–7, which we will discuss later.)

In the beginning of this passage, John sees a big angel holding a little scroll (see 10:1–7). Unlike the earlier scroll John had seen (see 5:1), this smaller one is open. Wrapped in a cloud with a rainbow over his head, this angel's face shines like the sun. His legs are like pillars of fire. With one foot on the sea and one on the land, his voice is like thunder. The angel swears

a solemn oath and declares that there will be no more delay; "the mystery of God" is about to be fulfilled. Time's up! "The mystery" seems to be a reference to the establishment of the kingdom of God. The seventh angel will soon blow his trumpet and the kingdom of this world will become the kingdom of our Lord and of his Christ, and he shall reign forever and ever (see 11:15).

A voice from heaven tells John to go to the big angel and "take the scroll" that is open in his hand (see 10:8). Approaching the enormous angel, John asks that the scroll be given to him. But the angel says he must "*take*" it. What's more, he must "eat it" (10:9). Similar to the earlier experiences of Jeremiah (see Jer 15:16) and Ezekiel (see Ezek 3:1–3), John eats the words of God: "It was sweet as honey in my mouth, but when I had eaten it my stomach was made bitter" (10:10). With the Word of God inside him, he is given a command: "You must again prophesy about many peoples and nations and languages and kings" (10:11).

Two Witnesses

Few passages in the Bible are more difficult to interpret than Revelation 11:1–14. John is given a measuring rod and told to measure the temple of God, the altar, and those who worship there. But he is *not* to measure the court of the Gentiles, which is outside the temple: "Leave that out, for it is given over to the nations, and they will trample the holy city for forty-two months" (11:2). Apparently, while the place of worship (the temple) is under the watchful eye and protection of God, the unmeasured area outside is not. This place is where unbelievers trample the holy things of God and disregard his invitation to turn from their evil ways. But more importantly, this area outside the temple is precisely the place where God's witnesses are to carry on their work.

All Christians are called to be witnesses and are sent into the world to testify to the truth of Jesus and the salvation found only in his name (see

Luke 24:48; Acts 1:8). But witnessing in this world is dangerous and must be done in the face of open hostility. The remainder of this passage introduces us to the "two witnesses." John is not only telling their story but also holding them up as examples of what it means to bear witness for Jesus in a hostile environment.

The two witnesses are clothed in sackcloth and described as "olive trees" and "lampstands" (11:3–4). They have supernatural powers that enable them to spew fire from their mouths, to stop rain from falling, to turn water into blood, and "to strike the earth with every kind of plague" (11:5–6). But their chief ministry is to bear witness to the truth. A demonic figure named "the beast" rises out of the bottomless pit, attacks them, and kills them (11:7). Rather than mourning the death of these divine emissaries, people in the city break out in celebration—even exchanging gifts for the occasion (see 11:9–10). However, after their dead bodies lie in the street for three and a half days, God raises them from the dead and takes them bodily into heaven in the sight of all their enemies (see 11:11–12)! In that very hour, a great earthquake destroys one-tenth of the city, and 7,000 people die (see 11:13). What can this possibly mean?

Though many commentators want to make the two witnesses into historical persons (Moses and Elijah, for example) and insist that the city is a specific geographical locality (Jerusalem), I am hesitant to impose such a specific application on the text. It seems to me that chapters 10–11 are intended to be more of a symbolic expression of how Christians are to witness to the truth while living in an evil and hostile environment. Numerous indications in the text itself encourage such a symbolic approach.

For one thing, when John wrote the book of Revelation (c. AD 90), *the temple* was no longer standing. So when he measured "the temple" and counted the "worshipers" (11:1), he was clearly thinking of a more spiritual reality, probably using his description as a metaphorical way of talking about the church as the newly constituted people of God. The reference to *42 months* (i.e., 1,260 days or 3½ years) is surely symbolic (see also 11:2–3;

12:6; 13:5). But what does it symbolize? Though many have labored long and hard to respond to this question, there is simply no consensus on the answer. We probably will never know for sure.

The fact that the two witnesses are called "lampstands" (11:4) is a further indication that this passage is intended to be read symbolically. We have already seen how the image of a lampstand is a metaphor for the churches (see 1:20). Recall that two of the seven churches (Smyrna and Philadelphia) were blameless, so perhaps the two witnesses stand for that part of the church that has never compromised the truth and remains faithful, even "unto death" (2:10).

A final indication of the metaphorical nature of this passage is seen in how *the city* where the two witnesses ministered is described. Though the city is clearly designated as the place "where their Lord was crucified," the author stops short of identifying it as Jerusalem. Rather, he calls it "Sodom" and "Egypt" (11:8). Apparently, John has a bigger "city" in mind than the literal Jerusalem.

Be My Witnesses

Revelation 10:1–11:14 seems to be John's call to the church to be witnesses—a sort of Great Commission according to the book of Revelation. Eating the scroll (see 10:1–11) must be seen in conjunction with being a witness (see 11:1–14). When we look at both passages together, we begin to see what is involved in being effective witnesses in an evil and hostile world.

First, we must *eat the book*. There can be no authentic witness to Christ and the coming Kingdom until someone eats the Word of God (see 10:8–11). You are what you eat. Hitler fed on Nietzsche. Stalin fed on Marx and Engels. Luther fed on Paul's epistle to the Romans. Notice that John has to *take* the scroll. It is not spoon-fed to him. He takes the Word, chews the Word, savors the Word, swallows the Word, and then digests the Word. He eats the parts he understands, and he eats the parts he doesn't! Though it is sweet in his mouth, it has a bitter aftereffect. "But solid food is for the mature, for those who have their powers of discernment trained by constant practice to distinguish good from evil" (Heb 5:14).

Second, once you assimilate God's Word into your very being, you are ready to *proclaim the Word*. Though the text makes a distinction between John, who eats the Word (see 10:1–11), and the two witnesses, who proclaim the Word (see 11:1–14), the thematic thread that holds them together is their mutual commitment to the Word. John eats the book so that the two witnesses can "prophesy" (11:3). A witness is not someone who shares his ideas and opinions. He is not even someone who recounts his own spiritual experience. Rather, being a witness involves sharing with others what you have eaten and digested from the Word of God. Typically, a witness will discover two realms of activity where he is called to serve: measuring and assessing the temple and the people of God (see 11:1–2) and evangelizing the unbelievers in the wicked city (see 11:4–14). Both areas desperately need voices that will clearly proclaim the Word of truth.

Third, to be an effective witness, you must *lay down your life*. To be a witness of Jesus Christ is to incur the fury of the Beast and to invite the hatred of the world. The Greek word for witness is *martus*, from which we derive the term "martyr." In the early church, saying to be a witness and to be a martyr were two ways of saying the same thing.

Jesus stated the matter succinctly in Acts 1:8—"But you will receive power when the Holy Spirit has come upon you, and you will be my witnesses in Jerusalem and in all Judea and Samaria, and to the end of the earth." Though we are not all called to be preachers and missionaries, we are all called to be witnesses. Notice how this mandate is profoundly simple and simply profound:

- "*You…*" Jesus is not talking about a special assignment for a select group of highly gifted saints. No, the call to witness is a privilege extended to all.

- "*Will be...*" The command is to *be* something, not to *do* something. Witnessing relates more to who we are than to what we do. Unfortunately, it is possible to "do witnessing" and at the same time be a bad witness!

- "*My...*" The whole point of witnessing is to direct people to Jesus. We are witnesses of him! While many seem to think of witnessing in terms of "giving my testimony," that is really secondary to the essential task of simply telling others about Jesus. The goal is to draw attention to him—not ourselves.

- "*Witnesses...*" When translated "You shall be my martyrs," we begin to understand the cost involved in naming his Name in a hostile world.

- "In *Jerusalem and in all Judea and Samaria, and to the end of the earth.*" Our witness must always begin at home (Jerusalem). But as we are faithful there with those we know and love the most, we are called to move outward in expanding concentric circles of influence, taking the name of Jesus to the ends of the earth.

- "*When the Holy Spirit has come upon...*" We simply cannot obey Jesus' call in our own strength. To be effective witnesses requires Pentecostal power!

As followers of Jesus Christ, we, too, are called to be witnesses, to be lights in the darkness, proclaimers of truth in a world of lies. We are called to share with others the Word we have eaten and digested. And our work is to be carried out in an evil city, hostile to the Name we bear. This is our primary task, our essential mission. Though we may find ourselves at times involved in helping the poor or the sick, participating in a Bible study, or serving on some committee devoted to good works, our primary calling is not there. No, our mission is to be witnesses of Jesus, bolding proclaiming the Word of truth wherever he calls us to serve.

For Reflection and Discussion

1. "You are what you eat." How does this saying explain our culture? Our church? Our family?

2. Describe your Bible study routine. Do you "eat" the Word? Savor it? Swallow it? Digest it?

3. What is the difference between "doing witnessing" and "being a witness"?

4. Do you regard martyrdom as strange and foreign to the gospel or integral to it?

5. What is the relationship between witnessing and the infilling of the Holy Spirit?

8.

Cosmic Christmas

(Rev 12:1–17)

The Gospel of John handles the Christmas story very differently than the other Gospels. Matthew and Luke tell the traditional story of Mary and Joseph in Bethlehem, the manger, the shepherds, and so on. But in John's account we have a different perspective on what was really happening that night when Christ was born. Rather than giving the historical facts of the story, John presents the theological meaning:

> In the beginning was the Word, and the Word was with God, and the Word was God.… The light shines in the darkness, and the darkness has not overcome it.… He was in the world, and the world was made through him, yet the world did not know him… And the Word became flesh and dwelt among us, and we have seen his glory.… (John 1:1, 5, 10, 14)

John helps us to understand that Jesus is so much more than a localized person in time and space. Though Jesus' ministry on earth involves healing sick bodies and opening blind eyes, there is a much larger dimension to what is happening. Jesus' life and ministry, though localized in time and space, has a cosmic dimension! We see this in startling clarity in Revelation 12.

At first glance, it does not look like the story of Christmas at all! But look more closely, and you discover all the essential elements of the story—without the localized specificity of time and place. We might say that Revelation 12 is Christmas from God's point of view: cosmic Christmas. The events occur not in Bethlehem, but in "heaven" (v 1). The time of the events described is unclear. Is John talking about something that happened in the past? Something that is happening now? Or perhaps something yet to occur? In *this* Christmas story, time and space are unimportantt.

Especially when we examine the characters in John's story do we begin to see the outlines of a "Christmas" narrative. First, we notice a godly woman giving birth in very unusual circumstances (vv 1–2). Next, we meet this woman's baby boy, who is destined to rule the nations (v 5). A fiendish adversary is also part of this story, whose single obsession is to kill that baby boy (v 4). However, God is watching over that precious baby to protect him and ensure that he grows to be a man and fulfills his glorious destiny (v 5).

That should sound familiar. Though John is writing about timeless events occurring in heavenly places, the contours of the Christmas story are clearly there: a godly woman, a divine child, and an evil monster intent on destroying the baby. But why does Pastor John want his first-century congregation to understand this cosmic dimension of the coming of Christ to the world? I can think of two very good reasons.

First, Pastor John wants his readers to be aware of the spiritual warfare that occurs whenever God's people are present in this evil world. Our real struggle in life is only superficially related to hostile governments, unbelieving neighbors, other religions, or economic hardships. Our real battle is not against flesh and blood "but against the rulers, against the authorities, against the cosmic powers over this present darkness, against the spiritual forces of evil in the heavenly places" (Eph 6:12).

Second, John wants Christians in the early church to know what happens to the woman in the story. While the Gospels focus on the life of Jesus and say little about the woman who gave him birth, Revelation 12 focuses more attention on the woman and gives only brief mention of her baby. Why? Because by this time everyone knew what became of that baby. He grew to be a man, gave his life on a cross, was raised from the dead, and now reigns as King of kings and Lord of lords (see 1:7; 9:11–16)! Revelation 12 tells us the rest of the story.

The Child

Though this passage makes only a few brief comments about the child who was born, they are important. His male gender is emphasized as well as the prophetic announcement that he is "to rule all the nations with a rod of iron" (v 5). These words are sufficient to indicate that this child is the promised Messiah (see also Ps 2:9; Rev 2:27; 19:15). We are told nothing about his life, ministry, or death on a cross. We read only that after he was born he was "caught up to God and to his throne" (v 5),[12] a reference to Christ's ascension (see Acts 1:9–11). Obviously, John has another purpose in mind than to tell the story of Jesus' life, death, and resurrection. Though the child disappears from the story, we know he'll be back. And when he comes the next time, every eye will see him (see 1:7). In the meantime, in Revelation 12, John's primary focus is on the woman and the dragon.

The Woman

The woman in John's story represents far more than Mary, the mother of Jesus. Clothed with the sun, with the moon under her feet, and wearing a crown of twelve stars on her head (v 1), this is a woman of amazing pedigree. But who is she? She seems to be a symbol of the people of God, the new Israel, the church. Just as Israel gave birth to Jesus, so the people of God now give birth to other offspring (v 17). In sharp contrast to the great prostitute (Babylon) that we will meet later in Revelation, the godly woman being attacked by the dragon is a picture of the church, the Bride of Christ. From chapter 12 through the end of the book of Revelation, this woman is preparing for her wedding day.

---

12 The term "caught up" (snatched up) is the same term used in 1 Thessalonians 4:17 to describe the "Rapture" of the saints.

The Dragon

Give free rein to your sanctified imagination as John describes the dragon in vivid detail (vv 3–4). He is enormous in size and red in color. He has seven heads, ten horns, and seven crowns. He uses his great tail as a weapon of mass destruction. This hideous monster has one passionate purpose: to devour the baby the moment he is born. However, thanks to the intervention of God, the dragon's plans are frustrated.

The plot thickens when John shares some important background information about this great, red dragon (vv 7–12). It is difficult to determine whether the dragon's expulsion from heaven occurred before, during, or after his attempt to kill the baby, but the chronology has little impact on the story. The point is that this dragon has been in revolt against God since the beginning of time. Apparently referring to the rebellion in heaven when Lucifer led perhaps a third of the angels in revolt against God (Rev 12:4; Ezek 28:12–17; Isa 14:12–15; Luke 10:18), John describes the climactic moment when this fiendish traitor and all his demonic minions are ignominiously cast out of heaven forever (see vv 7–9). Falling to earth, the dragon is furious because "he knows that his time is short" (v 12).

It is instructive to notice the names John uses to designate this great, red dragon. His names reveal his true identity (see vv 9–10):

- The *ancient serpent*. John's first-century readers would immediately recognize this term as a reference to the snake in the Garden of Eden (see Gen 3:1).
- The *devil* is a term that comes from the Greek *diabolos*, meaning "to accuse" or "to slander."
- *Satan* means "adversary."
- The *deceiver of the whole world* (v 9).
- The *accuser*. One of the most effective ways this evil being works against God is to bring charges against his children—day and night.

Looking at the names and descriptions of this evil dragon, we gain a clear understanding of his strategy in the war he is waging against the saints (see 12:17; 13:7). And when you know your enemy's tactics, it becomes very easy to defeat him (see 2 Cor 2:11). Satan's strategy is diabolically clear: deceive (v 9), condemn (v 10), and intimidate (vv 12, 17).

- *Deception.* Ever since the serpent tempted Eve in the Garden, Satan's primary tactic has been to tell lies, half-truths, and fabrications. "Did God really say, 'You shall not eat of any tree'?" he asked Eve. "You will not die!" (see Gen 3:1, 4). Thank God that his Word of truth equips us both to recognize the devil's deceptive ways and to counteract his lies.

- *Condemnation.* Like an expert prosecuting attorney, Satan is always gathering evidence to show what sinful, miserable failures we are. Unless we find a better attorney, we don't have a chance against him. Fortunately, we have an advocate with the Father: Jesus (see 1 John 2:1–2; Rom 8:1, 33–35).

- *Intimidation.* Satan is filled with fury "because he knows that his time is short" (12:12). But don't be fooled by his hideous looks and bullying threats. His ferocity is only a front to camouflage his despair: he knows his doom is sure.

How to Overcome

Pastor John tells the story of the dragon and the woman not only to acquaint his readers with information about cosmic realities but also to encourage the little flock he pastors to know how to survive and thrive in the evil empire where they are living. As a loving shepherd, he wants his sheep to know three things.

First, *the world is a battlefield, not an amusement park.* The dragon has declared war on all of God's children (see 12:17; 13:7). Therefore, if you are a member of the family of God seeking to do his will in this world, don't be surprised when all hell breaks loose!

Second, *your life has cosmic significance.* As Christians living in a hostile environment, it is often easy to draw the conclusion that our lives are making no impact on the course of human history. Pastor John wants the members of his congregation to understand that their lives are part of a much bigger reality. In fact, the future of the world is being determined by the humble obedience of the people of God. Your life matters!

Third, *you can overcome.* Verse 11 outlines three essential keys for living a victorious life: "They have conquered him [the dragon] by the blood of the Lamb and by the word of their testimony, for they loved not their lives even unto death."

- *The blood of the Lamb*—The Lamb of God's atoning sacrifice on the cross means that our sins can be forgiven and our hearts cleansed; as a result, Satan's accusations and condemnations lose their power (see Rom 8:1).

- *The word of their testimony*—Victory is possible only when our witness is public, when we boldly confess with our lips to the world around us that "Jesus is Lord" (see Rom 10:9–10).

- *The willingness to be a martyr*—The dragon is conquered when we are no longer intimidated by his bullying threats to kill us (see Luke 12:4–5; 1 Cor 15:55). What if he does kill us? We still win!

Few people better understood the nature of this cosmic battle we find ourselves in than Martin Luther. The words to his hymn "A Mighty Fortress" capture well the call to arms being issued to every child of God.

A mighty fortress is our God, a bulwark never failing;
Our helper He, amid the flood of mortal ills prevailing:
For still our ancient foe doth seek to work us woe;
His craft and power are great, and, armed with cruel hate,
On earth is not His equal.

Did we in our own strength confide, our striving would be losing;
Were not the right Man on our side, the Man of God's own choosing:
Dost ask who that may be? Christ Jesus, it is He;
Lord Sabaoth, His name, from age to age the same,
And He must win the battle.

And though this world, with devils filled, should threaten to undo us,
We will not fear, for God hath willed His truth to triumph through us:
The Prince of Darkness grim, we tremble not for Him;
His rage we can endure, for lo, his doom is sure,
One little word shall fell him.

That word above all earthly powers, no thanks to them, abideth;
The Spirit and the gifts are ours through Him who with us sideth:
Let goods and kindred go, this mortal life also;
The body they may kill: God's truth abideth still,
His kingdom is forever.[13]

For Reflection and Discussion

1. How does Revelation 12 help you to better understand Christmas?

2. What has this lesson taught you about Satan (the dragon)?

3. What has this lesson taught you about the church (the woman and her offspring)?

4. Which of Satan's tactics (deception, condemnation, or intimidation) has been used most often against the contemporary church? Which tactic has been used most often against you?

5. Describe a situation in your life right now where you feel attacked. How can Revelation 12:11 help you to be an overcomer in that situation?

---

13 Martin Luther, *"A Mighty Fortress"* (1529), trans. Frederic H. Hedge (1853).

9.
Cursèd Trinity
(Rev 13:1–18)

In his book *People of the Lie,*[14] psychiatrist Scott Peck tells a disturbing story about one of his patients, a teenage boy named Bobby who was struggling with depression. As he probed to discover the cause of his depressed condition, Dr. Peck learned that the boy's brother had recently committed suicide with a .22 caliber rifle. Thinking he had discovered the source of the young man's depression, he probed further. To his shock and horror, he discovered that the boy's parents had taken the rifle the brother used to kill himself, wrapped it as a present, and given it to Bobby for Christmas! Little wonder he was depressed.

As a psychiatrist, Dr. Peck had been trained to recognize a wide range of human aberrant behaviors. He was schooled in the art of diagnosing whether a behavioral dysfunction was the result of a neurosis, psychosis, phobia, chemical imbalance, emotional disturbance, or learning disability. But nothing in his training had prepared him for this! None of his psychiatric categories seemed quite to fit these parents or to explain their behavior. He finally realized that the only category that seemed to fit was one for which his training as a psychiatrist had not prepared him at all: *evil.*

In a secularized, sanitized, politically correct culture like America, it is seldom permitted to label anyone's actions as "evil." And yet there are some forms of human behavior for which no other language seems adequate. Revelation 13 (and its prequel, chapter 12) is a good place to begin for someone who has trouble believing in the existence of evil. It could serve as a basic text in a course entitled "Evil 101."

---

14 M. Scott Peck, *People of the Lie: The Hope for Healing Human Evil* (New York: Simon & Shuster, 1983), 47–69.

To do its worst, evil must look its best. Vice must masquerade as virtue. A suicide weapon must be wrapped as a Christmas present. Satan is the master of disguise. He can do nothing original. Therefore, for evil to succeed, it must appear as something good. The wolf must wear sheep's clothing (see Matt 7:15). Deceitful ministers must take the appearance of apostles of Christ (see 2 Cor 11:13). Satan must disguise himself as an angel of light (see 2 Cor 11:14). To do his worst, the devil must look his best! Nowhere is this more diabolically true than in Satan's attempt to duplicate the Holy Trinity. Because the true God is triune (Father, Son, and Holy Spirit), the prince of darkness mimics God by manifesting himself in a triune display of evil: Satan, Antichrist, and False Prophet.

Revelation 12–13 gives the clearest presentation in all of Scripture of this cursèd trinity. In Revelation 12, we see how the great, red dragon is the chief mastermind behind each and every expression of evil in the world. Having "seven heads and ten horns" (12:3), he is described as "that ancient serpent, who is called the devil and Satan, the deceiver of the whole world" (12:9). Day and night, before the throne of God, Satan accuses God's people of sin (see 12:10). Having lost his battle against God in heaven (see 12:7–9), and having been unsuccessful in his effort to destroy the baby boy birthed by the woman clothed with the sun (see 12:1–6), Satan now leads the effort to harass and destroy all the offspring of the woman, those who make up the church (see 12:17). In this sense, Satan is a demonic imitation of God the Father.

Chapter 13 introduces us to the other two members of this trifold expression of darkness: the beast rising out of the sea, the Antichrist, is a demonic imitation of God the Son (see 13:1–10), and the beast rising out of the earth, the False Prophet, is a diabolical effort to replicate God the Holy Spirit (see 13:11–18).

The Beast from the Sea (Rev 13:1–10)

Daniel 7 is indispensable background material for understanding the beast that John sees rising out of the sea. Daniel sees not one but four beasts coming from the sea, and the fourth one especially captured his attention because "it was different from all the beasts that were before it, and it had ten horns" (v 7). Looking more closely at these horns, Daniel sees yet another, smaller horn arise, which replaces three of the previous horns. This "little horn" has eyes and a mouth speaking great things (v 8). Discovering that the first three beasts represent a progression of three earthly kingdoms, Daniel learns that the fourth beast represents a kingdom "which shall be different from all the kingdoms, and it shall devour the whole earth, and trample it down, and break it to pieces" (v 23). As for the little horn that replaced the three horns, Daniel learns that it represents a king that "shall be different from the former ones, and shall put down three kings. He shall speak words against the Most High, and shall wear out the saints of the Most High" (vv 24–25). Daniel's vision also includes the sure and certain promise that "one like a son of man" will come with the clouds of heaven and be victorious over all these evil beasts and wicked tyrants, and the glorious kingdom he establishes will last forever (see vv 13–14).

Turning to Revelation 13, we can now more easily see the many parallels that exist between the vision of John and that of Daniel centuries earlier. John apparently expects us to understand that the beast coming out of the sea (see 13:1–10) is none other than the "little horn" of the fourth beast in Daniel's vision. This beast will rule over a global empire on the earth and, like the little horn in Daniel, his kingdom will be "different" from all the other worldly governments that have gone before. This seems to be the point that John wants to emphasize to his first-century congregation. The beast from the sea is coming to wage all-out war against the saints of God. His power and authority will be unequaled in the history of the world.

Examining other passages in the New Testament helps us to determine that this beast from the sea is none other than the "Antichrist," also known as "the man of lawlessness" (see 1 John 2:18, 22; 2 Thess 2:3–4, 7–10). In a fiendish effort to duplicate the second person of the Holy Trinity, the beast from the sea masquerades as Jesus Christ himself. Because the true Word of the true God became flesh and lived among us (see John 1:14), Satan will attempt to incarnate himself in the person of this evil world ruler. Tragically, millions will be fooled and will give him their allegiance and worship.

John graphically describes this blasphemous seducer who will lead the whole world astray:

- It has ten horns, seven heads, and ten diadems on its horns and blasphemous names on its heads (see 13:1).
- Merging the first three beasts of Daniel's vision into one horrific creature, John sees a creature that is like a leopard, like a bear, and like a lion (see 13:2).
- Satan (the dragon of chapter 12) gives this beast enormous power and authority to rule over the world (see 13:2).
- The beast is a gifted and powerful orator but uses his powers of speech to utter "haughty and blasphemous words" (see 13:5–6).
- This beast's rule is of relatively short duration: 42 months (see 13:5).
- The most notable characteristic of the beast is that one of its heads seemed to have been mortally wounded, but then it is miraculously healed. The "whole earth marveled" at this demonic imitation of a resurrection and began to worship the beast as well as the dragon who gave him his power (13:3–4).

It is noteworthy that the only ones on earth who refuse to worship this beast are those whose names are written in the Lamb's Book of Life (see 13:8). This, of course, infuriates the beast, who makes war against the saints and is allowed "to conquer them" (13:7). Pastor John is warning his flock that things are going to get much, much worse: "Here is a call for the endurance and faith of the saints" (13:10).

The Beast from the Earth (Rev 13:11–18)

So far we have seen two members of the cursèd trinity: Satan as the counterfeit "Father" and Antichrist as the counterfeit "Son." But who is the third member of this trifold expression of evil? The answer is found in the vision John has of the beast rising out of the earth (see 13:11–18). Again, give free rein to your sanctified imagination as John paints a graphic description of this horrible creature:

- It has two horns "like a lamb" but it speaks "like a dragon" (13:11).
- It has all the authority of the first beast (see 13:12).
- Similar to the Holy Spirit, whose purpose is to exalt the risen Lamb and prompt others to worship him (see John 15:26; 16:14), this beast from the earth "makes the earth and its inhabitants worship the first beast, whose mortal wound was healed" (13:12).
- It performs amazing signs and wonders (fire from heaven, etc.) and thus "deceives those who dwell on earth" (13:13–14).
- Making a statue of the first beast (Antichrist), it breathes life into the image so that it speaks (see 13:14–15)! This miracle seals the complete union of church and state so that politics and religion become inseparable.
- It causes everyone to be marked on the right hand or the forehead with "the mark, that is, the name of the beast or the number of its name" (13:16–17). This mark (the number 666)[15] is necessary for all economic transactions.

---

15 The number 666 has caused voluminous and passionate discussion for 20 centuries! To what or to whom does it refer? In both Hebrew and Greek, the letters of the alphabet can be used as numbers so that each letter has a numerical value. This means that names can be turned into numbers. Many attempts have been made to determine which names in history could possibly be made to fit the number 666. With a little ingenuity, this has been tried with names such as Nero, Caligula, Mohammed, Martin Luther, Oliver Cromwell, Napoleon, Hitler, etc. The possibilities are endless. It is interesting to note that 777 can be considered a perfect number, and the name Jesus in Greek is the number 888, one step above perfection. So perhaps the number 666 belongs to someone who is one step below perfection, a trinity of imperfection, a triple loser.

As the beast rising out of the sea (the Antichrist) exerts his power through politics and intimidation, the beast rising out of the earth (the False Prophet) exerts his power through religion and deception.

Look again at this cursèd trinity and notice how Satan, Antichrist, and the False Prophet are a demonic counterfeit of the Father, Son, and Holy Spirit of biblical orthodoxy.

- The Antichrist has a pseudo resurrection (see 13:3, 12, 14).
- The False Prophet is lamb-like and performs signs and wonders (see 13:11, 13–15).
- Both Satan (the dragon) and the Antichrist are worshiped (see 13:4, 8, 12–15).
- The Antichrist does his work during 3½ years, approximately the same amount of time of Jesus' ministry (see 13:5).
- The False Prophet is a sort of Minister of Propaganda for the Antichrist, exalting him and urging people to worship him, similar to the way the Holy Spirit exalts Jesus (see 13:12).
- As the saints were sealed by a mark on their foreheads (see 7:3–4; 14:1; 22:4), so the False Prophet marks all those who belong to Satan (see 13:16–18).

Treasures of Darkness

The prophet Isaiah tells of a promise God gave to the pagan king Cyrus that can be an encouragement to us in our study of Revelation: "I will give you the treasures of darkness… that you may know that it is I, the LORD, the God of Israel, who call you by your name" (Isa 45:3). Though darkness may frighten us and make us want to run to the light, there are treasures to be found in the dark places for those who have the wisdom and courage to ask God for help. Chapters 12–13 of Revelation introduce us to what undoubtedly will be the darkest period in human history. When the Antichrist rules the earth through a one-world government and the False

Prophet orchestrates a global religion, the powers of darkness will function at their maximum intensity. But John encouraged his flock with this message: God has told us in advance what will happen and exposed the lies and deceptions of those who want to lead us astray. Final victory belongs to the Lamb and all those who are his.

What words of counsel does Pastor John offer as he shares his vision, anticipating a future filled with demonic forces engaged in warfare against the people of God?

First, *be balanced*. Satan and his minions are real and powerful foes, but their doom is sure. In fact, they have already been defeated, and they know it! Therefore, we need to be vigilant and wise and yet not overly anxious. Be alert to your enemy, but never give him more attention than he merits.

> *There are two equal and opposite errors into which our race can fall about devils. One is to disbelieve in their existence. The other is to believe and to feel an excessive and unhealthy interest in them. They themselves are equally pleased by both errors and hail a materialist or a magician with the same delight.*[16]

Second, *don't be fooled*. Satan and his team (Antichrist and False Prophet) are all imposters, pretenders, and counterfeits. Like little monkeys, they can only imitate and produce ridiculous counterfeits of the work of the Father, Son, and Holy Spirit. "He who sits in the heavens laughs; the Lord holds them in derision" (Ps 2:4). The situation would be comical if the outcome were not so serious.

Third, *be steadfast and persevere* (see v 10). Pastor John's interest in foretelling the future is governed by his love for the sheep of his congregation. He knows things are about to get rough—really rough—and he is preparing his flock so they can survive and thrive in the evil day.

---

16   C. S. Lewis, *The Screwtape Letters* (New York: HarperOne, 1942), ix.

Fourth, *be prepared for battle*. Yes, warfare is coming. But you know the enemy's battle plan and, therefore, have no need to fear. Keep watch, and stand firm! "No weapon that is fashioned against you shall succeed.... This is the heritage of the servants of the LORD and their vindication from me, declares the LORD" (Isa 54:17).

For Reflection and Discussion

1. What can Christians do to find treasures in the darkness?
2. How will your Christian life be different because of what you have learned here?
3. What has been your attitude toward Satan in the past? How has this study affected the way you think about Satan and his work in the world?
4. The writer of Revelation repeatedly calls members of the body of Christ to be "overcomers," yet he writes that the saints would be "conquered" (see 13:7). How can both of these statements be true?
5. Describe how you feel about a one-world government.
6. Why is Satan such a copycat? Is evil capable of genuine creativity or must it always work in counterfeits?

10.

The Grapes of Wrath

(Rev 14:1–16:21)

Though many contemporary pastors seem hesitant to preach on the wrath of God, Pastor John had no such compunction. Knowing it was part of his sacred duty as a shepherd of God's flock, John lovingly but candidly explained in graphic detail just what the coming judgment would look like. His purpose was not to use "scare tactics" to coerce people into a response but rather to honestly set forth the truth about the future.

Jonathan Edwards had a similar purpose when on July 8, 1741, in a church in Enfield, Connecticut, he preached his famous sermon, "Sinners in the Hands of an Angry God." As a proper New England clergyman who read his manuscripts, Edwards was no hell-fire pulpit-pounder. His purpose in this sermon was simply to help his congregation understand what happens to those who refuse the grace of God. The sermon text was taken from Deuteronomy 32:35: "Vengeance is mine, and recompense, for the time when their foot shall slip; for the day of their calamity is at hand, and their doom comes swiftly." Though calmly reading the sermon manuscript, Edwards produced a dramatic and emotional response among his listeners (weeping, fainting, convulsing, etc.).

> *The God that holds you over the pit of hell, much as one holds a spider...is dreadfully provoked: his wrath towards you burns like fire.... O sinner! Consider the fearful danger you are in: it is a great furnace of wrath, a wide and bottomless pit, full of the fire of wrath, that you are held over in the hand of that God... You hang by a slender thread, with the flames of divine wrath flashing about it, and ready every moment to singe it, and burn it asunder.*

While some will want to debate the pastoral sensitivities involved in knowing how, when, and where to "preach the terrors," no one can debate the simple fact that the Bible clearly states there will be a day of unimaginable wrath and torment for everyone who refuses to worship the Lamb. In Revelation 14:1–16:21, we begin to understand the final destiny for those who have received the mark of the Beast. We also learn what will happen to those who have refused that demonic mark and have been sealed by God and marked on their foreheads by his name.

A New Song

Revelation 14 opens with a glorious vision of the Lamb standing on Mount Zion surrounded by 144,000 men and women who have his name and his Father's name written on their foreheads. They have refused the mark of the Beast and have chosen to be sealed by God instead. They are singing, and the sound of their united voices is like thunder, like the roar of many waters. The most amazing feature of this worship service is that the song being sung is a *new*[17] song: "No one could learn that song except the 144,000 who had been redeemed from the earth" (14:3). Not even the angels could join in the music, having themselves never known what it is like to be redeemed from sin! This is a song that only blood-bought sinners can sing.

Angelic Messengers

John sees three angelic messengers, one after another, flying through the heavens, each with a special announcement for citizens of the earth (see 14:6–13). The first angel flew "directly overhead, with an eternal gospel to

---

17 Two words in New Testament Greek are rendered "new" in English. *Neos* refers to time, something recent. Interestingly, this word is not used in Revelation at all. *Kainos* refers to quality, something that is fresh and vitally alive. This is the word John uses over and over in Revelation to describe a new name (2:17; 3:12), a new Jerusalem (3:12; 21:2), a new heaven and earth (21:1), and a new song (5:9; 14:3).

proclaim to those who dwell on earth, to every nation and tribe and language and people" (14:6). In what appears to be a final opportunity to accept redeeming grace, this angel extends a universal invitation to get right with God before it is too late: "Fear God and give him glory, because the hour of his judgment has come" (v 7). It appears there will be a final explosion of evangelistic activity during the last days, when the whole world will be given one final opportunity to believe the good news of salvation. Jesus spoke of this period of global outreach in these words: "And this gospel of the kingdom will be proclaimed throughout the whole world as a testimony to all nations, and then the end will come" (Matt 24:14).

The second angel has a more sobering message. No longer inviting people to believe in Jesus, this angel simply comes with the announcement that God's final judgment has begun: "Fallen, fallen is Babylon the great" (14:8). We will learn more about this wicked city and her fate in coming chapters. Here, we simply are told that her doom has come.

The third angel's announcement (see 14:9–13) underscores both the intensity of the torment of God's wrath and the finality of his judgment. There is no court of appeals!

> If anyone worships the beast and its image and receives a mark on his forehead or on his hand, he also will drink the wine of God's wrath, poured full strength into the cup of his anger, and he will be tormented with fire and sulfur in the presence of the holy angels and in the presence of the Lamb. And the smoke of their torment goes up forever and ever.... (14:9–11)

But John wants believers who are living on the earth during these tumultuous times to remember that a very different future is promised to those who trust in the Lamb:

> And I heard a voice from heaven saying, "Write this: Blessed are the dead who die in the Lord from now on." "Blessed indeed," says the

Spirit, "that they may rest from their labors, for their deeds follow them!" (14:13)

A Worldwide Harvest

John then sees a picture of a worldwide harvest (see 14:14–20). On numerous occasions, the Bible describes the final judgment in such terms. For example, Jesus' parable of the weeds (see Matt 13:24–30, 36–43) describes the end of the age as a time of harvest. Jesus explains that God is letting the good grain and the weeds grow in the same field together "until the harvest." Then he will tell the reapers to gather the weeds to be burned but gather the wheat to be stored in his barn.

In Revelation 14:14–20, John also pictures a great harvest at the end of the age. In John's vision, the one responsible for actually doing the harvesting is seated on a white cloud, "like a son of man, with a golden crown on his head, and a sharp sickle in his hand" (14:14). This is clearly a reference to Jesus himself. An angel comes out of the temple in heaven and announces in a loud voice; "Put in your sickle, and reap, for the hour to reap has come, for the harvest of the earth is fully ripe" (14:15). In one majestic statement, using an astonishing economy of words, the text describes the climactic moment of human history in the simplest manner possible: "So he who sat on the cloud swung his sickle across the earth, and the earth was reaped" (14:16). Apparently, this refers to that part of the harvest when the saints are gathered together into the storehouse of God for safe-keeping (see Matt 24:30–31).

Another angel with another sickle is then summoned to complete the harvest (14:17–20). Receiving a command that is similar—but very different—from the first, he is told: "Put in your sickle and gather the clusters from the vine of the earth, for its grapes are ripe" (14:18). This angel then swings his sickle over the earth and gathers in a harvest of grapes, which are thrown immediately into the great winepress of the wrath of God. And the winepress was trodden outside the city, and blood flowed from the winepress, as high as a horse's bridle, for 1,600 stadia [about 184 miles] (14:19–20).

It is this graphic image of the winepress of God's wrath that inspired Julia Ward Howe to write "The Battle Hymn of the Republic" (1861):

Mine eyes have seen the glory of the coming of the Lord,
He is trampling out the vintage where the grapes of wrath are stored;
He hath loosed the fateful lightning of His terrible swift sword–
His truth is marching on.

Seven Golden Bowls

Just when one thinks the final judgment can't get any worse, we discover there is yet more to the story. Revelation 15–16 describes the next part of John's vision. He sees seven angels who are given seven golden bowls. Each bowl is full of the wrath of God (15:7). The seven bowls (16:1–21) need to be seen in conjunction with the seven seals (see 6:1–17; 8:1–5) and the seven trumpets (see 8:6–9:21; 11:15–19), which also describe the wrath and judgment coming upon the world. One by one, the contents of these bowls (seven plagues) are poured upon the earth. With this final manifestation of God's fury, "the wrath of God is finished" (15:1):

1. The first bowl (16:2), when poured out on the earth, produces painful canker sores on everyone who bears the mark of the Beast.
2. The second bowl (16:3) is poured into the sea, which makes the salt water become "like the blood of a corpse," causing the death of every living thing in the sea.
3. The third bowl (16:4–7) is poured into the rivers and springs, turning the fresh water into blood. An angel explains that it is only fair that the worshipers of the Beast should be forced to drink blood because "they have shed the blood of saints and prophets" (16:6). The punishment fits the crime.

4. The fourth bowl (16:8–9) is poured on the sun so that its heat is greatly intensified, and it scorches people like fire. This is "global warming" with a vengeance! Yet rather than repenting and turning back to God, the sufferers only harden their hearts and curse his name.

5. The fifth bowl (16:10–11) is poured directly "on the throne of the beast" itself, plunging his kingdom into darkness. Though people gnaw their tongues in anguish, they still refuse to repent.

6. The sixth bowl (16:12–16) is poured out on the Euphrates River so that it dries up, making possible an invasion of an enemy army from the east. The Dragon, Beast, and False Prophet conjure up three unclean spirits "like frogs" (16:13), which assemble a mighty army to withstand the invasion. The two armies meet and prepare for battle at a place called Armageddon.

7. The seventh bowl (16:17–21) is poured out into the air and releases the most cataclysmic series of disasters the world has ever seen! There are flashes of lightning, rumblings, peals of thunder, and a great earthquake. Islands disappear, mountains sink, and hailstones weighing 100 pounds fall from the sky. The great city of Babylon is destroyed, along with many other cities.

It makes us uncomfortable to contemplate God's coming wrath upon those who have refused his grace. Visions of an angry God disturb us and cause us to wonder if perhaps we have fully understood who this Lamb of God really is. And yet this, too, is part of the reality of our faith. Salvation and judgment always go together. If we deny the truth of coming wrath on sinful rebels, we will soon discover that we have no basis for affirming the truth of his coming salvation for repentant sinners.

Join the Choir!

Looking again at that heavenly choir we encountered at the beginning of our study (see 14:1–5), we learn what is involved in becoming a member of this heavenly chorus. It is almost as if Pastor John wants you and me to join the choir! But what are the requirements to become part of this heavenly choir?

1. *Experience redemption* (see 14:3). The word *redemption* literally means "to be purchased, bought." No one gets to heaven without a price first being paid for his or her soul: the blood of the Lamb (see 1 Pet 1:18–19; 1 Cor 6:19–20). To be purchased and redeemed by God means we are sealed, and we belong only to him (see 7:1–4; 22:4). We do not belong to the Beast! God has put his mark upon us, and the Lamb's name is written on our foreheads (see 14:1).

2. *Remain pure and blameless* (see 14:4–5). When John calls the members of the choir "virgins," it is doubtful he means it in the literal sense. Rather, he is referring to people who have received both forgiveness for all their sinful actions and cleansing for their sinful nature. Refusing to defile themselves through the love of this world (see 1 John 2:15–17; James 4:4), the redeemed know they are the Bride of Christ, preparing for their wedding day (see 2 Cor 11:2; Rev 21:9).

3. *"Follow the Lamb wherever he goes"* (14:4). When Jesus said, "Follow me" (Mark 1:17), he meant it! Being a Christian is not merely a positional change of our status in heaven. No, it is a daily walk with the living Lord. It is a personal relationship with Jesus Christ. "For all who are led by the Spirit of God are sons of God" (Rom 8:14).

4. *Tell the truth and be blameless* (see 14:5). Members of the Lamb's heavenly choir have rejected falsehood and lies in every form. They are blameless. The truth has set them free (see John 8:32), and they are therefore committed to a life of transparent integrity. Satan is

the father of lies and has been a liar from the beginning of time (John 8:44). He and his followers have no place in heaven (see Rev 22:15).

5. *Sing and worship the Lamb* (see 14:2–3). The supreme occupation in heaven is worship and praise. The song of the redeemed is new, not because it has been written recently but because it is always fresh and alive. And when they sing, though there are millions of them, they sing with one voice.

Wanna join the choir?

For Reflection and Discussion

1. When was the last time you heard a sermon about God's wrath? What was it like?

2. What are you doing to become involved in world evangelization in these last days?

3. Describe your personal reaction to biblical passages that depict God as an angry sovereign, pouring out his wrath on sinners. Does your concept of God fit with such passages? Why or why not?

4. The writer of Revelation wants us to be assured of our place in the choir of the redeemed. Are you confident of your place there?

11.

Up in Smoke

(Rev 17:1–19:5)

Again and again in the Bible, we discover that a "city" represents more than a sociological or geographical reality. Its meaning is profoundly theological. Though the Hebrew term refers to a guarded or fortified place, it originally was used as well to include a spiritual being that watched over the place, a sort of guardian angel. Jacques Ellul states the matter powerfully in his classic study on this topic:

> We must admit that the city is not just a collection of houses with ramparts, but also a spiritual power. I am not saying it is a being. But like an angel, it is a power, and what seems prodigious is that its power is on a spiritual plane. The city has, then, a spiritual influence. It is capable of directing and changing a man's spiritual life.[18]

In early biblical history, the spiritual influence of a city is uniformly negative. It is only when we are introduced to "the city of God" that we begin to discover a positive impact that is possible from life in "the city."

Cities in the Bible

After chapter 16, the book of Revelation focuses on two cities: Babylon, the city of man, and Jerusalem, the city of God. We might say that the climax of biblical history is "a tale of two cities." But before we begin, let's take a moment to acquaint ourselves with some of the biblical history of cities.

---

18 Jacques Ellul, *The Meaning of the City* (Grand Rapids: Eerdmans, 1970), 9.

It is noteworthy that the first city in human history, named *Enoch*, is built by the first murderer (Gen 4:16–17). Cain, trying to cope with his guilt over killing his brother, at first wandered aimlessly in the land of Nod. But rather than looking to God for comfort and fellowship, he built a fortress city and named it after his son. He hoped his little city would be a place of security, stability, and meaningful relationships.

The next city we meet in Scripture is *Babel* (Gen 11:1–9), which became the ultimate symbol of worldly evil and rebellion against God. Founded by Nimrod (Gen 10:8–11), Babel and its tower became proverbial for imperial power, human pride, manmade religion, and disregard for the commands of God. No other city in history became more associated with humanity's revolt against God than Babel, later called Babylon.

> *Babylon is not a city. She is the city…. No one can rival her, not even Rome. Not because of her historical greatness, but because of what she represents mythically. All the cities of the world are brought together in her; she is the synthesis of them all… She is the head of, and the standard for the other cities…Venice, Paris, New York—they are all the same city, only one Babel always reappearing….[19]*

Continuing our journey through early Hebrew history, the next cities we encounter are *Sodom* and *Gomorrah* (Gen 18:16–19:29). These two cities are notorious for their sin; indeed their names have become synonymous with a reprobate lifestyle. The Genesis account highlights their sexual perversions as the cause of their destruction, but the prophet Ezekiel mentions other sins as well:

> *Behold, this was the guilt of your sister Sodom: she and her daughters had pride, excess of food, and prosperous ease, but did not aid the poor and needy. They were haughty and did an abomination before me. So I removed them, when I saw it. (Ezek 16:49–50)*

---

19   Ibid., 20–21.

The wickedness of Sodom and Gomorrah was such that God had no option but to destroy them. They were beyond redemption!

Upon arrival in the Promised Land, God's people build a city of their own: *Jerusalem*. Although God approved the building of this city, its record is a strange mixture of good (see Ps 87:1–3; Isa 48:2) and evil (see Isa 1:21; Mic 3:10). Things in Jerusalem at times got so bad that she was compared to Sodom (Isa 1:10; Rev 11:8)! It is no accident that when Jerusalem eventually falls under divine judgment, her residents are sent into exile in Babylon (2 Kings 25:1–21; 2 Chron 36:17–21). Babylon "is truly the place of the genuine captivity of the church."[20]

The biblical record is clear: every city of man will fail. Though God's people live in these cities and seek their well-being (Jer 29:7), the cities themselves all will be destroyed. They are irredeemable. Only the city of God will last forever (see Rev 21–22).

> By faith, [Abraham] went to live in the land of promise, as in a foreign land, living in tents… For he was looking forward to the city that has foundations, whose designer and builder is God…. But as it is, they desire a better country, that is, a heavenly one. Therefore God is not ashamed to be called their God, for he has prepared for them a city…. (Heb 11:9–10, 16)

The Fall of Babylon

Revelation 17 begins when an angel who has one of the seven bowls of wrath invites John to come and witness the judgment that is about to fall on Babylon. Likened to a "great prostitute," this city is the epitome of wickedness and rebellion against God. John goes to great lengths to give a graphic description of this evil woman, now identified with her evil city (17:1–6). The scarlet beast on which she is seated has seven heads and

---

20 Ibid., 20.

ten horns and is covered with blasphemous names (17:3). It appears this wicked woman is in alliance with Satan himself (see 12:3). Dressed in purple and scarlet and adorned with jewels, she has a history of engaging in illicit sex with all the kings of the earth. She lives in extravagant luxury (see 18:7, 11–13), is involved in human trafficking (18:13), and practices sorcery (18:23). Her name is written clearly on her forehead for all to see: "Babylon the great, mother of prostitutes and of earth's abominations" (17:5). To culminate his description of this hideous woman, John notes that she is "drunk with the blood of the saints, the blood of the martyrs of Jesus" (17:6). We can summarize John's description of this evil woman Babylon by noting that she is seductive, immoral, powerful, rich, drunk, and has global influence. Above all, she hates Jesus and his followers.

But what city is John talking about? Where is it? And when does it appear in human history? The debate among scholars is fierce when it comes to identifying "Babylon" in terms of geopolitical human history. Though the reference to "seven mountains on which the woman is seated" (17:9) undoubtedly caused John's readers to think of Rome, the passage makes clear that first-century Rome cannot exhaust the meaning of what John is describing. The reference to "seven kings, five of whom have fallen, one is, the other has not yet come" (17:10) is notoriously difficult to interpret. Though many have tried to make John's prophecy fit a certain historical progression of Roman emperors in the first and second centuries, there is simply no unanimity concerning what John is writing about. What we can say with certainty is this: the woman and the city she rules derive their power from the scarlet beast on which she rides: Satan himself (see 12:3; 17:3, 7–8).

The forces of evil in the world, which seem united and strong, eventually will turn on one another and destroy themselves. Though feigning love for the woman, the kings of the earth in reality hate her and are just waiting for the right moment to revolt against her and destroy her. In doing so they unwittingly will carry out God's sovereign purposes (17:16–17).

Though the coalition of evil kings is divided concerning many things, there is one thing on which its members have total and complete unanimity: hatred of the Lamb and all those who follow him (17:13–14).

Though Babylon and the axis of evil powers allied with her seem invincible, don't be fooled. This wicked woman and all who do business with her are about to be destroyed. The Dragon will be defeated by the Lamb (see 17:14)!

Finally, John gives us a horrific depiction of the destruction of Babylon (see 18:1–24). Though describing a reality that is yet in the future, John sees it as if it is already an accomplished fact (18:1–3)! The only way to be saved from the judgment coming on this evil city is to "come out of her" (18:4). To remain in Babylon is to share in her destruction.

The fall of Babylon elicits wails of sorrow from all those who profited from her economy of wickedness and participated in her sensuous practices. Kings, merchants, and sailors (18:9–19) join in a loud lamentation of grief as they watch the city go up in flames. But looking at the words of their sorrow, we discover that these people are not really grieving the loss of someone they loved. Rather they are feeling sorry for themselves, lamenting all the riches and prosperity that they will no longer personally enjoy because of the fall of this wicked city.

In a final conclusive demonstration of what is happening, an angel takes a great millstone and throws it into the sea, saying: "So will Babylon the great city be thrown down with violence, and will be found no more" (18:21). Never again will the city of man experience the joy of music, craftsmanship, industry, or weddings. The lights of Babylon will be extinguished forever (18:22–23).

The Original Hallelujah Chorus

From heaven, saints and angels watch in rapt silence as Babylon the Great is destroyed and ignominiously tossed into the depths of the sea like

a great millstone. As the evil city sinks into the ocean of God's wrath never to be heard from again, a song of praise arises from the heavenly choir. This is the original *Hallelujah Chorus*!

In the New Testament, the word *hallelujah* occurs only here in Revelation 19 (vv 1, 3, 4, 6). It transliterates a Hebrew expression meaning "praise God," which appears often in the Old Testament. Everyone in heaven wants to join the choir at the victory of the Lamb over the evil woman, Babylon. One "Hallelujah!" is not enough. Four times, the word is shouted in praise because the great prostitute has finally been defeated. The Lord God Almighty is reigning in power, and the Bride is at last ready for her wedding day.

> After this I heard what seemed to be the loud voice of a
> great multitude in heaven, crying out,
> **"Hallelujah!**
> Salvation and glory and power belong to our God,
>   for his judgments are true and just;
> for he has judged the great prostitute
>   who corrupted the earth with her immorality,
> and has avenged on her the blood of his servants."
>   Once more they cried out,
> **"Hallelujah!**
> The smoke from her goes up forever and ever."
>   And the twenty-four elders and the four living creatures
> fell down and worshiped God who was seated on the throne,
> saying, "Amen. **Hallelujah!**" And from the throne came a
> voice saying,
>   "Praise our God,
>   all you his servants,
> you who fear him,
>   small and great."
>   Then I heard what seemed to be the voice of a great
> multitude, like the roar of many waters and like the sound of

mighty peals of thunder, crying out,
   "Hallelujah!
For the Lord our God
   the Almighty reigns.
Let us rejoice and exult
   and give him the glory,
for the marriage of the Lamb has come,
   and his Bride has made herself ready. (19:1–7)

George Frederick Handel got it right. Though most people have no trouble recognizing the *Hallelujah Chorus* that he wrote in 1741, they seldom remember the song that precedes it, yet the previous song sets the context for the eruption of praise we encounter in the *Hallelujah Chorus*. Just before the entire choir begins singing "Hallelujah!" a tenor voice sings a plaintive solo. The words are taken from Psalm 2:9, a prophecy about what will happen when the Messiah comes again to reign in power. The lyrics are short and to the point: *Thou shalt break them, thou shalt break them with a rod of iron; Thou shalt dash them in pieces like a potter's vessel.*

When the solo is finished, the entire choir stands on its feet and joins in loudly singing what may be the greatest choral piece ever written—the *Hallelujah Chorus*. Handel chose the lyrics from John's description of the praise that erupted in heaven when the city of Babylon was finally destroyed: a fourfold "Hallelujah!" celebrating the final victory of God (see 19:1–8). Taking additional lyrics from Revelation 11:15 and 19:16, Handel's *Hallelujah Chorus* is complete:

   Hallelujah! Hallelujah! Hallelujah! Hallelujah! (Rev 19:1, 3, 4, 6)
   For the Lord God omnipotent reigneth. Hallelujah! (Rev 19:6)
   The kingdom of this world is become the Kingdom of our Lord,
      of his Christ, And he shall reign forever and ever! (Rev 11:15)
   King of kings, and Lord of lords; Hallelujah! (Rev 19:16)

Visiteurs

My family and I had the privilege of living ten years as missionaries in the country of France. In our official papers, issued by the French government, our status was defined as *visiteur*. This meant that while we were not officially French citizens, we were permitted to reside there. Our passport defined our true national identity (American), but our residence was in France.

Such a situation describes the life of a Christian. Though we reside in the "city" of this world, our citizenship is elsewhere. The Bible encourages us to see ourselves as aliens and pilgrims, living as exiles in this city of man. We are in great spiritual danger when we begin to imagine that this world is our home and forget that our true citizenship is elsewhere.

To conclude this chapter, let me summarize John's words into four succinct commands addressed to the people of God, who find themselves living as exiles in Babylon:

1. *Babylon is seductive, so be careful.* Don't be fooled by the glitzy allure of the things of this world. Remember that Babylon is really a prostitute. Underneath the glitz, glamour, and industrial-strength mascara, she is nothing more than a whore. Don't be fooled by her charms and her feigned interest in your well-being!

2. *Babylon is cruel, so be brave.* Babylon is a murderous and evil monster. She hates you because you belong to the Lamb! She wants to kill you and consume you. But the day of her judgment is coming soon, so be brave!

3. *Babylon is doomed, so come out.* Babylon's destruction will be sudden, total, and irreversible. Therefore, "come out of her, my people, lest you take part in her sins, lest you share in her plagues" (18:4). Flee now, before it is too late! Flee the wrath to come! You can be *in* the world without being *of* the world. To be a friend of this world is to be an enemy of God (see James 4:4).

4. *Babylon will be replaced, so shout "Hallelujah!"* The singing in heaven is not taking delight at someone's punishment but rather the joyful response of the saints when justice is finally established in the earth and God's Name is vindicated. Babylon is a wicked prostitute. Her punishment is just and fair. But most importantly, her destruction prepares the way for the new Jerusalem, dressed in white, coming as a bride for her wedding day!

For Reflection and Discussion

1. This passage of Scripture urges us to think theologically about cities. What have you learned?

2. Scripture describes Babylon as a place of sex, money, drugs, luxurious ease, and hatred of Christians. Some say this describes modern American culture. Do you agree?

3. The Bible forbids us to love the world and worldly things but doesn't give many specifics about what this looks like. A previous generation associated worldliness with things like lipstick, movies, wearing jewelry, and so on. Today, what activities and possessions indicate that someone loves this world?

4. Scripture calls us to be *in* the world but not *of* the world (John 17:15–16). How has this chapter helped you to better obey this mandate?

12.

The Return of the King

(Rev 19:6–21)

The third volume of J.R.R. Tolkien's The Lord of the Rings series is titled *The Return of the King*. It recounts the climactic moment when Prince Aragorn returns and takes the throne that is rightfully his. One wonders if Tolkien may have been thinking of Revelation 19 when he chose the title for his final volume. When Jesus finished the work he had come to do during his earthly life as recorded in the Gospels, he promised his followers that he would come again to complete all that he had begun:

> *In my Father's house are many rooms. If it were not so, would I have told you that I go to prepare a place for you? And if I go and prepare a place for you,* ***I will come again*** *and will take you to myself, that where I am you may be also. (John 14:2–3, emphasis added)*

Indeed, the last recorded words of Jesus in the Bible are a promise he repeated three times: "I am coming soon" (Rev 22:7, 12, 20).

Donald G. Bloesch uses an analogy from World War II to help us better understand the two comings of our Lord. He compares the first coming to D-Day, June 6, 1944. This was the date Allied troops landed in Normandy, and it was the decisive battle of the war. Once that beachhead was secure, everyone knew that Germany's ultimate defeat was assured. However, many bloody battles would be fought before Germany finally surrendered on May 8, 1945. Bloesch makes the point that though Satan has already been decisively defeated by the first coming of Christ, he continues to fight: "Calvary signifies that the warfare is virtually, but not actually, over."[21]

---

21 Donald G. Bloesch, *Essentials of Evangelical Theology, vol. 2* (Peabody, MA: Prince Press, 2001), 205.

A story is only as good as its ending, and the gospel story ends with a glory more wonderful than any human could have ever imagined. Indeed, "eye has not seen, nor ear heard, nor have entered into the heart of man the things which God has prepared for those who love Him" (1 Cor 2:9 NKJV). From Revelation 19 to the end of the book, God gives us a sneak preview of how human history will end. He wants us to know the final outcome so that, as we continue to fight battles here on earth, we have the assurance that we are on the winning side. We are just part of a mopping up operation. The final victory is certain!

Once Babylon the Great has been destroyed (Rev 17–18), things move quickly and in a positive direction. Chapters 19–22 describe the final events of human history:

- The "Hallelujah Chorus" is sung and wedding invitations are sent out (19:1–10).
- The King of kings (the Groom) returns (19:11–16).
- The Antichrist and the False Prophet are defeated (19:17–21).
- Christ and his followers reign for 1,000 years (20:1–6).
- Satan is defeated and tossed into the lake of fire (20:7–10).
- The final judgment occurs before the great white throne (20:11–15).
- A new heaven and a new earth appear (chs 21–22).

The King of Kings Returns

The climactic moment of human history occurs when suddenly heaven opens and a mighty warrior appears riding on a white horse (19:11). His eyes are like fire, and he is wearing many crowns upon his head. He is clothed in a robe dipped in blood (vv 12–13). But he is not alone! He is accompanied by an enormous army also riding on white horses. Each rider is dressed in a white robe (v 14). Interestingly, the only weapon mentioned is the sharp sword that comes out of the mouth of the one leading the army of heaven (v 15).

But who is he? Who is this mighty warrior coming to establish his eternal kingdom and to marry his bride? By this point in the story, his identity should be evident to all. He is called "Faithful and True" (v 11), "the Word of God" (v 13), and "King of kings and Lord of lords" (v 16). John notes that he also has another name, but this name is a mystery "that no one knows but himself" (19:12). Though we can know Jesus truly and accurately, we can never know him exhaustively.

What a contrast there is between the first coming and the second coming of Jesus Christ!

Jesus' First Coming	Jesus' Second Coming
A tiny baby	A mighty warrior
Riding on a donkey	Riding on a white horse
In meekness and humility	In glory and power
He came to save	He comes to judge
He is seen by a few	He is seen by everyone
To shed his own blood	To shed the blood of his enemies
The Lamb of God	The Lion of Judah

The Antichrist and the False Prophet Are Defeated

The battle described in Revelation 19:17–21 is apparently the Battle of Armageddon, which was foretold in 16:13–16. However, this is not the last great battle of human history but the next-to-the-last battle, as we shall see in Revelation 20:7–10.

The battle is announced by an invitation to all the birds to come to "the great supper of God" (vv 17–18). In other words, scavengers are summoned to feed upon the carcasses that will soon litter the field of battle. What a dramatic contrast this is to "the marriage supper of the Lamb" (19:9)!

King Jesus and his army engage in conflict with the Beast (Antichrist) and the False Prophet, along with the kings of earth and their armies. The greatest battle in human history is described in two short verses. Interestingly, nothing is said about the weapons, strategy, or tactics used.

> *And the beast was captured, and with it the false prophet.... These two were thrown alive into the lake of fire that burns with sulfur. And the rest were slain by the sword that came from the mouth of him who was sitting on the horse, and all the birds were gorged with their flesh. (vv 20–21).*

Are You Ready for This?

Before we proceed to the conclusion of the book of Revelation, let's take stock of what the rest of the New Testament teaches us about the second coming of Christ. Examining these other references helps us to complete the picture we find in Revelation.

Christ's return will be *physical.* Some claim we should not be too literal in how we think about Christ's return but should rather imagine that Christ's second coming is only another way of talking about the new birth and spiritual regeneration. The second coming thus becomes a metaphor of hope, not something to be taken literally. But the New Testament says Jesus will return just as he ascended into heaven: in a physical bodily form (see Acts 1:9–11).

Christ's return will be *universally visible.* Though it is difficult to imagine how people on opposite sides of the globe will see him at the same time, the Bible insists that when Jesus returns, "every eye will see him" (Rev 1:7). All the nations of the earth will see him coming on the clouds (see Matt 24:30). No one will miss the reality of what is happening. Jesus himself told his disciples:

If anyone says to you, "Look, here is the Christ!" or "There he is!" do not believe it. For false christs and false prophets will arise and perform great signs and wonders, so as to lead astray, if possible, even the elect. See, I have told you beforehand. So, if they say to you, "Look, he is in the wilderness," do not go out. If they say, "Look, he is in the inner rooms," do not believe it. For as the lightning comes from the east and shines as far as the west, so will be the coming of the Son of Man. (Matt 24:23–27)

Christ's return will be *glorious*. Unlike his birth in a humble stable in Bethlehem, Jesus' return will be "in clouds with great power and glory" (Mark 13:26).

Christ's return will be *sudden* and *surprising*. The Scripture is clear that no one knows the day or hour of Christ's return, "not even the angels in heaven, nor the Son, but only the Father" (Mark 13:32). Thus, Christ's return will be surprising, "like a thief in the night" (1 Thess 5:2). Jesus compares his return to the days of Noah and the sudden coming of the flood. As "they were unaware until the flood came and swept them all away, so will be the coming of the Son of Man" (Matt 24:39).

Christ's return will be *final*. Though the last judgment will occur after Christ's return (see Rev 20:11–15), there is no biblical indication that people will have an opportunity to repent and be saved after he returns. In the parable of the ten virgins, Jesus explains that when the Bridegroom suddenly comes, some will be ready and others will not. Once the Bridegroom comes, the marriage feast will begin and the door will be shut (see Matt 25:1–13).

Christ's return will be *soon*. Three times in the last chapter of the Bible, Jesus says, "I am coming soon" (Rev 22:7, 12, 20). After 2,000 years of waiting, it may seem difficult to understand what he meant by the word *soon*. Though we should guard against the temptation to set dates, Jesus apparently wants us to live in a state of constant readiness.

*The doctrine of the Second Coming has failed, so far as we are con-
cerned, if it does not make us realize that at every moment of every year
in our lives Donne's question, "What if this present were the world's last
night?" is equally relevant.*[22]

Given the fact that Scripture wants us to anticipate his imminent return, how then should we live? What can we do to live in daily prepared-
ness for the Bridegroom's arrival?

First, we must *be wise and discerning.* Let no one lead you astray because many "false christs and false prophets will arise and perform great
signs and wonders" (Matt 24:24).

Second, we must *stand firm.* We can expect the persecution of
Christians to intensify, but "the one who endures to the end will be saved"
(Matt 24:13).

Third, we must *preach the gospel.* The preaching of the good news is to
continue throughout the world until Christ returns (see Matt 24:14).

Fourth, we must *discern the signs of the times.* Christ prohibits any attempt to fix the date of his return, but he urges us to watch for the signs of
his coming. Several of these signs are enumerated in Matthew 24.

Fifth, we must *be ready to meet him anytime and anywhere.* Just as a wise
homeowner takes precautions to protect his property against a surprise visit by a thief in the middle of the night, so Jesus urges his followers to live
in constant readiness for Christ's return (Matt 24:42–43). "Therefore you
also must be ready, for the Son of Man is coming at an hour you do not
expect" (Matt 24:44).

Charles Wesley wrote a powerful hymn on the second coming of
Christ, "Lo! He Comes with Clouds Descending" (1758). It would be difficult to find a more appropriate conclusion to this chapter than to quote
these words penned over two centuries ago.

---

22 C.S. Lewis, *The World's Last Night and Other Essays* (New York: Harcourt, 1952), 109.

Lo! He comes with clouds descending,
Once for favored sinners slain;
Thousand thousand saints attending,
Swell the triumph of His train:
Hallelujah! Hallelujah! Hallelujah!
God appears on earth to reign.

Every eye shall now behold Him
Robed in dreadful majesty;
Those who set at naught and sold Him,
Pierced and nailed Him to the tree,
Deeply wailing, deeply wailing, deeply wailing,
Shall the true Messiah see.

Now redemption, long expected,
See in solemn pomp appear;
All His saints, by man rejected,
Now shall meet Him in the air:
Hallelujah! Hallelujah! Hallelujah!
See the day of God appear!

Answer Thine own bride and Spirit,
Hasten, Lord, the general doom!
The new Heav'n and earth t'inherit,
Take Thy pining exiles home:
All creation, all creation, all creation,
Travails! groans! and bids Thee come!

The dear tokens of His passion
Still His dazzling body bears;
Cause of endless exultation
To His ransomed worshippers;
With what rapture, with what rapture, with what rapture
Gaze we on those glorious scars!

Yea, Amen! let all adore Thee,
High on Thine eternal throne;
Savior, take the power and glory,
Claim the kingdom for Thine own;
O come quickly! O come quickly! O come quickly!
Everlasting God, come down!

For Reflection and Discussion

1. What have you learned about the second soming that you did not know before this study?
2. Does the thought of Christ's return bring you comfort or fear?
3. Why do you think God does not disclose the date of Christ's return?
4. Review Matthew 24 and list some "signs of the times" that indicate we may be living in the last days before Christ's return.
5. What specific things can believers do now to ensure they "stay awake" and are prepared for the second soming?
6. What do you think Peter meant when he told believers to hasten the Lord's return (see 2 Pet 3:11–12)?

13.

The Final Exam

(Rev 20:1–15)

Few passages of Scripture are more contested than Revelation 20. Passions run hot concerning the order of events described in this passage, and often the debate turns bitter concerning how Christ's 1,000-year reign is to be understood. The word *millennium* comes from the Latin *mille* (thousand) and *annus* (year). This is the only passage in the Bible that speaks specifically on this subject. Here are some key questions that need to be answered as we seek to determine our own position on these matters:

- Are the 1,000 years to be understood literally or figuratively?
- Is John talking about the future or the present?
- Who will reign with Christ, and what will it look like?
- What is God's purpose in this millennial reign?
- Does Revelation intend to map out a chronology of the end times, or is the order of these events relatively unimportant?

There are basically three explanations for how this 1,000-year reign has been understood. One is the doctrine of *premillennialism*. The prefix "pre" means that Christ will come back *before* the millennium. This view teaches that the present age will end in a terrible time of great tribulation and suffering. Then Christ will return and establish a literal kingdom that will last 1,000 years, where believers will reign with him on the earth. Christ will be physically present on earth during this time, and Satan will be bound in the pit and thus have no influence. It will be a time of peace, and many will turn to the Lord. At the end of the 1,000 years, Satan will be loosed and join forces with those who have been only nominal in their faith. This position takes Revelation 19:11–22:6 as a basic chronology of how the end-time events will unfold. The more Christians are persecuted in today's world, the more this position grows in popularity.

Those holding to a premillennial position typically fall into two groups: those who believe in a pre-tribulation rapture and those who believe in a post-tribulation rapture. The former teach that believers will be raptured first and not experience the times of trial coming on the earth for a seven-year period. At the end of the tribulation, Christ will return with his saints to reign on the earth for 1,000 years. The latter teach that the rapture will occur only after believers have experienced the Great Tribulation.

A second school of interpretation is called *post-millennialism*. This view holds that Christ will return *after* a 1,000-year earthly reign of his saints. This position believes that the progress of the gospel and the growth of the church will gradually increase so that more and more people will become Christians and society will be increasingly "Christianized" until gradually the "millennial age" will emerge. Finally, Christ will return at the end of this happy period. This optimistic position believes in the power of the gospel to change the world. Many missionaries of the eighteenth and nineteenth centuries were of this persuasion. We can grasp something of the optimism of post-millennialism in the missionary hymn, "We've a Story to Tell to the Nations" by H. Ernest Nichol.

> *We've a story to tell to the nations,*
> *That shall turn their hearts to the right,*
> *A story of truth and mercy,*
> *A story of peace and light.*
> *For the darkness shall turn to dawning,*
> *And the dawning to noonday bright;*
> *And Christ's great kingdom shall come on earth,*
> *The kingdom of love and light.*[23]

---

23 H. Ernest Nichol, "We've a Story to Tell to the Nations," *The United Methodist Hymnal* (Nashville: United Methodist Publishing, 1989), 569.

A third perspective on end-times chronology is called *amillennialism*, which sees the millennium in non-historical, non-literal terms. Revelation 20:1–10 thus describes the present church age. Those saints who have died are already reigning with Christ in heaven, so amillennialists expect no earthly reign of God's people. There is no 1,000-year reign yet to come. Most amillennialists would not consider the 1,000 years to be a literal number but rather a symbolic reference to an unspecified, lengthy period of time. All the end time events described in the Bible (return of Christ, general resurrection, last judgment, new heaven and earth, etc.) will occur more or less at once.

Though I tend to favor a premillennial (post-trib) position, I hold my views humbly and without dogmatic fervor, believing that the emphasis of Scripture is not on the chronology of the end times but rather the spiritual readiness of God's people. I also recognize that the biblical data is somewhat ambiguous and therefore can be legitimately interpreted in various ways. Frankly, I do not pretend to be smart enough to figure it all out! Perhaps it is time to stop arguing over the recipe and just enjoy the meal!

Revelation 20 describes four important events that will occur before the final consummation of a new heaven and new earth. Let's look at these events one at a time, seeking to understand their meaning and application for us today.

Satan Is Bound (Rev 20:1–3)

After dealing with the Beast and the False Prophet (see 19:19–20), the Lord turns his attention to their leader, Satan. Reminding us of the names and history of this archenemy of God (dragon, ancient serpent, devil, Satan), John wants us to understand that this evil monster is no match for Jesus Christ. An angel seizes Satan, binds him with a great chain, and throws him into the abyss where he is locked up for 1,000 years. Once before, Satan had experienced a "fall" when he was cast from heaven to earth (see 12:7–12). This time, he experiences a second and more disastrous fall as he is cast from earth into the bottomless pit.

The stated purpose of Satan's confinement is not punishment; that will come later. Rather he is locked away "so that he might not deceive the nations any longer" (v 3). Therefore, any rebellious activity against God during this period will be the result of human arrogance and willful disobedience rather than temptation from the devil. A post-millennialist or amillennialist typically sees the binding of Satan as a reference to Jesus' first advent. Christ's presence on earth, and then the birth of the church, has placed clear limits on the extent of Satan's destructive influence. A premillennialist sees the binding of Satan in much more literal terms: our adversary will be rendered powerless during a 1,000-year earthly reign of Christ after his second coming.

The Reign of Christ (Rev 20:4–6)

Though Christ will reign on the earth during this 1,000-year period, he will not reign alone. But who are these people seated on thrones, reigning with him? In answer to this question, John specifically mentions the martyrs, those who have been killed because of their testimony on Jesus' behalf (v 4). Other New Testament passages speak of a future time when the saints will sit on thrones and play a role in the judgment of the world (see Matt 19:28; 1 Cor 6:2–3; Rev 3:21). This reign of the saints is not in heaven, but on the earth.

As this millennial kingdom comes to an end, "the rest of the dead" will be raised to life, an event John calls "the first resurrection" (vv 5–6). These saints are delivered from "the second death" and serve as priests and co-regents with Christ. A premillennial position sees these as literal events that will happen on the earth, while other views tend to think of the "first resurrection" as a reference to the new birth.

Satan Is Released to Be Punished (Rev 20:7–10)

Surprisingly, after his 1,000-year imprisonment, Satan is released "for a little while" (v 3). Once again, he will be at liberty to deceive the nations, gathering Gog and Magog (an apparent reference to all, or most of, the nations) to make war against the people of God and "the beloved city." But before the battle is even fought, fire comes down from heaven and consumes all the enemies of God. Satan is then thrown into the lake of fire, where the Beast and the False Prophet have already been consigned (see 19:20), to be tormented forever.

Why would God permit his archenemy to come back and again deceive people? This question has no easy answer. Perhaps God's purpose is to expose once and for all the utter perversity and rebellion of the human heart. Despite all of the tangible proofs of God's gracious goodness and victorious reign, many people will continue to refuse to bow the knee and give him their trust and allegiance!

The Last Judgment (Rev 20:11–15)

The dead are called to stand before the great white throne, and the books are opened to determine who will be cast into the lake of fire. The Book of Life is also opened. But who is the one seated on this great white throne of judgment? Is it God the Father or God the Son? This text doesn't say, but a case could be made for either answer. In view of the unity of God, quibbling over the matter seems unnecessary.

Those dead who were not part of the first resurrection (see 20:5–6) are now raised to life and "judged by what was written in the books, according to what they had done" (20:12). Jesus stated in the Sermon on the Mount, "You will recognize them by their fruits" (Matt 7:16). Here, at the last judgment, a person's actions during his life will reveal the truth about his character and his relationship with God. Salvation is by faith alone, but faith inevitably is manifested by the works it produces.

Death and Hades are then thrown into the lake of fire. Here we see the death of Death! Likewise, everyone whose name is not recorded in the Book of Life is thrown into the lake of fire. Remember what Jesus said:

> *Truly, truly, I say to you, whoever hears my word and believes him who sent me has eternal life. He does not come into judgment, but has passed from death to life. Truly, truly, I say to you, an hour is coming, and is now here, when the dead will hear the voice of the Son of God, and those who hear will live. (John 5:24–25)*

Living in Anticipation

The Bible clearly states that everyone has an appointment with death and after that comes judgment (Heb 9:27). This judgment will determine one of only two possible destinations for every human being: heaven or hell. Living in anticipation of that final judgment should help us to live better today.

> *The heavens will disappear with a roar; the elements will be destroyed by fire, and the earth and everything done in it will be laid bare. Since everything will be destroyed in this way, what kind of people ought you to be? You ought to live holy and godly lives as you look forward to the day of God and speed its coming. That day will bring about the destruction of the heavens by fire, and the elements will melt in the heat. But in keeping with his promise we are looking forward to a new heaven and a new earth, where righteousness dwells. (2 Pet 3:10–13, NIV)*

Awareness of the final judgment is meant to prompt us to live in godliness today. We should be quick to extend grace and forgiveness to those who may have hurt us. Christ's soon return should motivate us to evangelize our neighbors while there is still time to accept God's gracious offer of salvation. Yes, a day of reckoning is coming soon. Each of us will stand before the Judge of all the earth and be called to give an account for the lives we have lived. Such an awareness should prompt everyone to ask the following questions:

- *Do I have a good Lawyer?* John said, "I write this to you so that you will not sin. But if anybody does sin, we have an advocate [i.e., a legal representative] with the Father—Jesus Christ, the Righteous One" (see 1 John 2:1 NIV).
- *Is there unconfessed sin in my life?* To live in willful, continual, habitual sin is a dangerous way to live! If we hope to escape the wrath of God, we cannot continue to carry the burden of unconfessed sin (see I John 1:9).
- *Am I trusting in the Lamb's finished work of redemption on the cross?* We must trust in Christ's good deeds, not our own, to save us. He paid a debt he did not owe so we could receive a gift we do not deserve. "There is therefore now no condemnation for those who are in Christ Jesus" (Rom 8:1).

For Reflection and Discussion

1. Have you struggled with trying to understand the timetable of end-time events? How has this study affected your perspective?

2. Describe your own understanding of the 1,000-year reign. What are the practical implications of your belief?

3. When did you last hear a sermon on the last judgment? Why do you think this part of Scripture is so seldom taught or preached about?

4. Do you live in anticipation of the final judgment? Are you confident of where you stand with Christ and what will happen to you?

5. What does this statement mean to you: "If you are born once, you will die twice; but if you are born twice, you will die once"?

14.
The City of God
(Rev 21:1–22:5)

In our postmodern world, one encounters a wide range of ideas about what happens when we die. Some believe in *annihilation* (when you die, you cease to exist). Others opt for *reincarnation* (you will return to earth as another creature or plant) or perhaps *universalism* (everyone will go to a better place). Some hope for a halfway house (purgatory, limbo) that exists somewhere between heaven and hell. But these are false teachings that may make people feel better in the short term but lead to disaster in the long term. Like drinking alcohol while trapped in a blizzard may make a freezing person feel warm, "it is false warmth. People have been known to freeze to death feeling warm."[24]

Even among Christians today, many have notions of heaven that have no biblical support at all. Some think in terms of disembodied spirits floating forever on clouds, playing harps. Others imagine that heaven will be a painfully long church service, a never-ending singalong in the sky, one praise chorus after another. Peter Kreeft tells the story of an English vicar who was asked what he expected after death. He replied, "Well, if it comes to that, I suppose I shall enter into eternal bliss, but I really wish you wouldn't bring up such depressing subjects."[25]

Fortunately, the book of Revelation gives us an authoritative picture of that place the redeemed will one day call home. It is important to note that John sees heaven coming *down* to us on the earth rather than us going *up* to heaven (see 21:2, 10). Both heaven and earth have been made new! In

24 Rebecca Price Janney, *Who Goes There?: A Cultural History of Heaven and Hell* (Chicago: Moody, 2009), 13.

25 Peter Kreeft, *Everything You Ever Wanted to Know about Heaven...But Never Dreamed of Asking* (San Francisco: Ignatius Press, 1990), 196.

Greek, the word for "new" describes something in respect to quality, not in respect to time. John is not saying this reality he is describing is a recent phenomenon but rather that it has a quality and nature that are different from anything yet known to man.

A Description of Heaven

Overwhelmed by the glory of what he sees, John struggles to describe the indescribable. He begins by telling us what is *absent* from this new city of God:

- No more sea (see 21:1)
- No more death (see 21:4)
- No more mourning or crying (21:4)
- No more pain (see 21:4)
- No temple (see 21:22)
- No sun or moon (see 21:23)
- Nothing unclean (see 21:27)
- No more curse (see 22:3)
- No more night (see 22:5)

The challenge of describing the city of God to those who live in the city of man is similar to the challenge of describing Miami Beach to an indigenous native who has never traveled far from his home in the far north of the Americas. To speak of palm trees, white sand, and surf boards makes little sense to those who have never seen such things. But to say, "There are no icebergs, snow, or polar bears in that fair land," immediately communicates! John begins his description of the city of God by telling his readers of things that they know well in this world but will be absent in the world to come.

John then describes what is *present* in this glorious city. Dressed as a bride for her wedding day, the New Jerusalem is resplendent in beauty and purity (see 21:2, 9–11). The walls of the city are 200-feet thick (or tall?)

and are transparent, "like clear glass" (v 18). Because all of Jerusalem's enemies have been defeated, the wall is not necessary for protection. Rather, it shows the glory of the city and designates those who are "in" from those who are "out." The twelve gates of the city are named for the twelve tribes of Israel and each gate is made of a single pearl (vv 12–13, 21). The twelve foundations are layers of precious stones, each named for one of the twelve apostles (v 14). The main street of the city is made of pure gold (v 21). The gates are never shut so that all nations can enter (vv 24–27).

Perhaps the most remarkable thing about the city of God is its shape. Being 1,400 miles long, wide, and tall, it is in the form of a cube. There is only one other structure in the Bible that has this shape: the Holy of Holies (1 Kings 6:20). Indeed, "the dwelling place of God is with man" (21:3).

Although the old Jerusalem had no river, the New Jerusalem has "the river of life" running through the middle of the city (22:1–2; see Ps 46:4; Ezek 47; Zech 14:8). Reminding the reader of the Garden of Eden, this river springs from the throne of God and gives life to all who drink from it. On the banks of the river is "the tree of life" (22:2). Since Adam and Eve's expulsion from Eden, no humans have been permitted to eat from this tree (see Gen 3:22–24), but now this fruit is freely available to all. Furthermore, the leaves of this tree bring healing to the nations (22:2). In powerfully symbolic ways, the New Jerusalem appears as a new Eden, where the people of God finally rediscover their true home.

Life in this glorious city marks a new beginning for God's redeemed humanity. The biblical story of redemption is not ending; it is just getting started! This may be the end of the book, but it is *not* the end of God's redemptive story. Now the real story can begin, and God's people can at last be all they were created to be and do all they were created to do! At the end of The Chronicles of Narnia, C. S. Lewis closes the lengthy narrative (seven volumes) with lines that could easily apply to the New Jerusalem.

And for us this is the end of all the stories, and we can most truly say that they lived happily ever after. But for them it was only the beginning of the real story. All their life in this world and all their adventures in Narnia had only been the cover and the title page: now at last they were beginning Chapter One of the Great Story which no one on earth has read: which goes on forever: in which every chapter is better than the one before.[26]

Will You Be Happy in Heaven?

Not everyone will be happy in the kind of place John is describing. Heaven is a prepared place for prepared people. Only those who are thirsty for righteousness (see 22:6), have lived a life of victory on earth (see 22:7), and have their names written in the Lamb's Book of Life (see 21:27) will be allowed entrance. Nothing unclean will be permitted in the Holy City (see 21:27). John is explicit about who will not be allowed in the New Jerusalem: the cowardly, the faithless, the detestable, murderers, the sexually immoral, sorcerers, idolaters, and all liars (see 21:8; 22:15).

In his final meal with his disciples, Jesus explained that he was going away to "prepare a place" for them, so that where he was going they could come too (John 14:1–3). Are *you* prepared for that place prepared for you? Will *you* be happy in heaven?

Will you be happy in a place of constant worship and praise? Though heaven should not be conceived as "sitting in church forever," John's picture of heaven reminds us that to see God face-to-face (see 22:4) is to worship him forever.

Will you be happy in a place where all is purity and light? Nothing impure will be allowed in the city of God. Because there is no night there and the walls are made of transparent glass, there will be no place

---

26 C. S. Lewis, *The Last Battle* (New York: HarperCollins, 1956), 210–211.

to hide in heaven. Only those who love the light will be happy there (see John 3:19–21).

Will you be happy in a place of reconciling love? In heaven, we will be surrounded by men and women from every imaginable ethnicity, nationality, and socioeconomic group. The citizens of the New Jerusalem may well include persons who have hurt you or those you love. Heaven will be a miserable place for someone nurturing a grudge, harboring hatred, or holding racist attitudes.

Will you be happy in a place where doing the will of God is man's highest joy? Those in the New Jerusalem serve God forever by doing that which is pleasing to him. For those who have not devoted their lives on earth to doing God's will, heaven may be an unhappy experience, because doing the will of God is what heaven is all about (see Matt 6:10; 7:21; 12:50).

For Reflection and Discussion

1. How do you envision heaven? Has this study caused you to revise your thinking?
2. Recall conversations you've had with people who held false notions about life after death. What might you do to correct their thinking?
3. Our grandparents often sang about heaven, but contemporary worship seldom mentions it. Why do you suppose this is so?
4. How does thinking about your eternal destiny affect the way you live today?
5. Call to mind someone who loves light and truth. Now call to mind someone who loves darkness and secrecy. How do they behave differently? Which person do you think will feel most "at home" in heaven?
6. Imagine being face-to-face with God. How do you feel about that prospect? Do you have that kind of open, honest relationship with God now?

15.
The Last Word
(Rev 22:6–21)

When someone is nearing death, their final words usually reveal that about which they feel most deeply.

- Nathan Hale (1776): "I only regret that I have but one life to give for my country."
- Lord Nelson (1805): "Thank God, I have done my duty."
- Socrates (399 BC): "Crito, I owe a rooster to Asclepius. Will you remember to pay the debt?"
- Dominique Bouhours (French grammarian, 1702): "I am about to—or I am going to—die; either expression is used."
- Oscar Wilde (1900): "Either this wallpaper goes, or I do."
- John Wesley (1791): "The best of all: God is with us."
- Jesus (AD 33): "Father, into your hands I commit my spirit!" (Luke 23:46).

Revelation 22:6–21 records God's final words to us, at least as they are presented in the Bible. It would be misleading to think that these words take priority over other words God has spoken, but they do underscore what is important to him and what he wants us to remember. These words complete what he desires for us to understand about life and salvation. Looking back, these last words of God affirm and authenticate all that has been said before by reminding us that "these words are trustworthy and true" (22:6). Looking forward to the future, these words give us a triple promise: "I am coming soon!" (22:7, 12, 20).

A Word of Blessing

As we saw in the Introduction, seven blessings or "beatitudes" appear in the book of Revelation. Two of them are in this final passage. First, the Lord says, "Blessed is the one who keeps the words of the prophecy of this book" (22:7). If we understand the book of Revelation simply as a timetable for the last days, we miss its greatest significance. Rather, God exhorts us to live as overcomers *today* as we anticipate what lies ahead. Trust in the Lamb; love your neighbor; resist temptation; keep your doctrine pure; obey his commands; bear witness to the truth; stand fast in tribulation; be faithful unto death; and live daily in the hope of that glorious moment when the kingdoms of this world will become the Kingdom of our Lord and of his Christ. Then he shall reign forever and ever. Yes, blessed are those who keep these words!

God's final beatitude says, "Blessed are those who wash their robes, so they may have the right to the tree of life and that they may enter the city by the gates" (22:14). The Greek verb translated "wash" is in the present tense, which indicates a continual washing. Once is not enough. God's blessing on our lives comes when we learn to wash our robes in the blood of the Lamb every day. In Revelation 7:14, a different verb tense was used. There, the redeemed are described as those who "have washed their robes and made them white in the blood of the Lamb." Both verbs ("washed" and "made white") are in the aorist tense, signifying an action that is done once and for all. To be forgiven for our outward sinful behaviors and cleansed from our inward sinfulness requires *both* a once-and-for-all act of trusting in the finished work of Calvary *and* a daily trust in the ongoing cleansing necessary to remain blameless, holy, and pure.

A Word of Command

For the second time, John cannot resist the impulse to worship the messenger rather than the one who sent the message (see 22:8, 19:10). He is rather like a teenager who receives a love letter in the mail and so falls in love with the mailman! With a gentle but firm rebuke, the angel tells him: "You must not do that!…Worship God" (22:9). These words apply not only to John but also to us. If the study of the book of Revelation does not lead us to worship and praise God, we have missed the point! Theology must always lead to doxology.

A Word of Warning

These final verses of Revelation contain a fourfold warning. As we anticipate the future God has prepared for our world, it is good to remember that the fear of the Lord is the beginning of wisdom (see Prov 9:10).

1. "Do not seal up the words of the prophecy of this book, for the time is near. Let the evildoer still do evil, and the filthy still be filthy, and the righteous still do right, and the holy still be holy" (22:10–11). The day of grace will end soon, and then everyone will remain forever what he or she really is! It will be too late to reform your ways and find God's favor and grace. Therefore, repent now, while there is still time. The day is coming soon when redemption will no longer be possible. Your destiny will be fixed, for good or for bad—forever.

2. "I am coming soon, bringing my recompense with me, to repay each one for what he has done" (22:12). Everyone will stand before God, and his works will be examined. For the righteous, there will be great reward and blessing. For the wicked, there will be judgment and condemnation. Sinners may run, but they can't hide. "Be sure your sin will find you out" (Num 32:23).

3. "Outside are the dogs and sorcerers and the sexually immoral and murderers and idolaters, and everyone who loves and practices falsehood" (22:15). It is sobering to realize that many will be excluded from God's presence forever. Those who refuse to confess their sins and repent will find themselves in a place of eternal torment and absolute despair (see 14:9–11).

4. "I warn everyone who hears the words of the prophecy of this book: if anyone adds to them, God will add to him the plagues described in this book, and if anyone takes away from the words of this prophecy, God will take away his share in the tree of life and in the holy city, which are described in this book" (22:18–19). Some, claiming to believe the Bible, want to add scriptures of their own (the Koran, the Book of Mormon, the "Gnostic Gospels," etc.). Others try to take away portions of the Bible that don't fit their worldview. God gives a terrifying warning to both: don't mess with my Word!

A Word of Invitation

Revelation ends with two beautiful invitations that reassure us of God's infinite grace. The first invitation comes from the Holy Spirit and the church and is addressed to everyone everywhere:

> *The Spirit and the Bride say, "Come." And let the one who hears say, "Come." And let the one who is thirsty come; let the one who desires take the water of life without price. (22:17)*

For everyone hearing these words, regardless of their circumstances, it is not too late! The door of grace is still open. Come! Some say that "the altar call" or "the invitation" is an invention of American evangelicalism and unknown in the previous history of the church. Not so! "The invitation" is as old as the New Testament itself. Come! Receive grace and put your trust in the Lamb. But understand that this is the final call. Come now—before it's too late!

The second invitation, however, comes not from heaven but from the earth. In the first invitation, God invites his people to come to him. But then the roles are reversed. The redeemed on earth—millions of them—invite God to come to them. "Come, Lord Jesus!" (22:20). First expressed in 1 Corinthians 16:22, this is one of the earliest prayers of the church. The Greek imports a word from Aramaic to preserve the original intensity of the plea: *Maranatha!* Come, Lord Jesus! The Bride is ready and longs to consummate the union. Christ will return only when his Bride longs for his arrival with passionate intensity. Come, Lord Jesus!

The Last Word

But wait. There is yet one final word. All the previous words have been penultimate (next to last). This word is the ultimate and final word for all people, in all times, everywhere. When this word is said there is truly nothing else to say. I'm talking about the very last word in the biblical text: *Amen.*

Transliterated from Hebrew into both Greek and English, the term comes from a root word that means "firm, dependable, secure, and certain." To say "Amen" means, "I agree and affirm and accept as true all that has been said."

When the last word in the Bible is *Amen,* God is affirming that all he has said is true and all he has promised will surely come to pass. Jesus Christ is the guarantee and authenticator of it all. In fact, Jesus *is* God's Amen (Rev 3:14).

In [Jesus] it is always Yes. For all the promises of God find their Yes in him. That is why it is through him that we utter our Amen to God for his glory. (2 Cor 1:19–20)

When worshipers say "Amen," they mean: "Yes. I agree. Let it be so. All has been said." There is no more fitting conclusion to this study of the book of Revelation than for me to invite you to join this mighty affirmation of all that God has said and done and promised to do. So go ahead, shout a loud and heartfelt, "Amen!"

For Reflection and Discussion

1. We noted in the first chapter that John's book is not just a revelation *from* Jesus but a revelation *of* Jesus. Reflecting upon your study, would you agree?

2. Have you ever seen or heard someone tampering with God's Word, either adding to it or taking from it? How did you feel? What did you do?

3. As a whole, does the book of Revelation fill you with hope or dread? Does the prayer, "Come, Lord Jesus!" seem natural for you?

4. Has this study changed the way you think about worship? How?

5. Would you recommend the study of Revelation to a friend who is seeking Jesus Christ? Why or why not?

CPSIA information can be obtained
at www.ICGtesting.com
Printed in the USA
LVOW04s0841121115

462001LV00004B/3/P

9 781593 177959